risen, ascen

Martin Dudley was born in Birmingham and
educated at King Edward's School. He studied
theology at King's College, London, and has
a doctorate in theology. Ordained in Wales, he
has served suburban, rural and new housing
estate parishes, and is now Rector of the
Priory Church of St Bartholomew the Great,
Smithfield, in the City of London. A Fellow
of the Society of Antiquaries and of the Royal
Historical Society, he also serves on the Professional Conduct and Complaints Committee
of the Bar Council.

risen, ascended, glorified

Meditations
for the Days from
Easter to Trinity

MARTIN DUDLEY

Published in Great Britain in 2002 by
Society for Promoting Christian Knowledge
Holy Trinity Church
Marylebone Road
London NW1 4DU

British Library Cataloguing-in-Publication Data

A catalogue record for this book is available from
the British Library

ISBN 0–281–05387–1

Typeset by Pioneer Associates, Perthshire
Printed in Great Britain by
Omnia Books, Glasgow

CONTENTS

SOURCES AND FURTHER READING

Biblical quotations are generally from the Revised Standard Version of the Bible © 1946, 1952 and 1971, though some are from the New Revised Standard Version of the Bible © 1989, both versions by the Division of Christian Education of the National Council of the Churches of Christ in the USA. Used by permission. All rights reserved. Occasionally quotations are paraphrased.

St John Chrysostom, *Homilies on the Gospel of St John and the Epistle to the Hebrews* (Grand Rapids, Eerdmans, reprinted 1978).

K. T. Keim, 'On Judas', quoted in Cheyne and Black, *Encyclopedia Biblica* (London, A & C Black, 1901, vol. 2, col. 2628).

Catherine of Siena, *The Dialogue*, tr. S. Noffke (New York, Paulist Press, 1980).

Unattributed quotations in the text generally come from one of the sources below.

Many of the liturgical texts quoted here can be found in pre-Vatican II missals and breviaries. I used *The Missal in Latin and English* (London, Burns, Oates and Washbourne, 1952). Among the older books on the Easter liturgy, much is to be gained from Louis Bouyer, *The Paschal Mystery* (London, George Allen & Unwin, 1951) and Aemiliana Löhr, *The Great Week* (London, Longmans, 1958). Hymns are normally quoted from *Hymns Ancient & Modern, Revised*.

The writings of Cécile Bruyère and Prosper Guéranger are to be found in Sister Mary David Totah's volume *The Spirit of Solesmes* (Tunbridge Wells, Burns & Oates, 1997).

The *Forty Gospel Homilies* of St Gregory the Great are published by Cistercian Publications, 1990. John of Ford, *On the Song of Songs* was also published by Cistercian Publications, in 1982.

Of the many books on St Thomas Aquinas, one of the best is by James Weisheipl, OP: *Friar Thomas d'Aquino: His Life, Thought and Works* (Oxford, Basil Blackwell, 1975).

For a discussion of the paintings of Jan Van Eyck, see Craig Harbison, *Jan Van Eyck: The Play of Realism* (London, Reaktion Books, 1991).

Magdalena the Sinner by Lilian Faschinger was published by Hodder Headline, 1997.

There are many translations of *The Imitation of Christ* available. Further insight into the spiritual culture of the time can be found in John van Engen's translation of devotional texts entitled *Devotio Moderna: Basic Writings* (The Classics of Western Spirituality, 1988).

On Corpus Christi, see Miri Rubin, *Corpus Christi: The Eucharist in Late Medieval Culture* (Cambridge, Cambridge University Press, 1991).

Information about St Bartholomew the Great can be found on www.greatstbarts.com.

THE EASTER VIGIL
This is the night

Christ dies. Daylight flees. Darkness comes. The Temple's double veil is rent. The earth quakes. The dead come forth and speak with the living. Christ is laid in the tomb; the stone is sealed, the guard set. 'In this darkness Life and Death are waging a grievous battle; one is destroying the other, and no one will know who has won, until daybreak on Sunday.'

Holy Saturday is a day without liturgy, a marked contrast to Maundy Thursday and Good Friday. In most churches it is a day of preparation. The activity – the arranging of flowers, the setting out of vestments, the assembling of the materials for the fire – is directed towards a celebration that is expected. An old Latin prayer asks God to grant 'that we who await the resurrection of your Son with faithful expectation may participate in the glory of his resurrection'.

Late into the night or very early on Easter morning a new fire will blaze in the darkness. The great Paschal Candle will be lit. 'Lumen Christi' sings the minister who carries it in procession: The light of Christ. And the faithful reply: 'Deo gratias' – thanks be to God. We know, of course, that the darkness of Good Friday will give way before the light of Easter Day, but the cry of thanksgiving remains a heartfelt one. If we have participated in the liturgy of Holy Week, shared with Christ the agony and desolation of the Passion and have waited, as he waited, for the glory of the resurrection, then our thanksgiving for the light comes from the very depth of our being.

The great Paschal Vigil, the new fire, the Paschal Candle,

and the Prophecies, are not a celebration of the empty tomb. Its discovery – even though we hear of it during the vigil – does not come until the dawn. What we celebrate in the night hours is Christ's resurrection. It is known to us on the first Easter morning but it actually happens in advance of its discovery, in much the same way that being pregnant precedes the visible signs of conception and future birth. The event is, therefore, not the same as the discovery that the event has taken place. In the darkness before the dawn we celebrate the profound mystery of the resurrection of the one who was crucified. It is the mystery that stands at the centre of our faith: we believe that Jesus Christ suffered under Pontius Pilate, was crucified, dead and buried, and that on the third day, according to the reckoning of days from evening to evening, he rose again.

This is no ordinary statement. Death is a dissolution of the elements that make for life, a separation of the spiritual and material elements. It is an experience common to all mortals. We can speak of death because we have seen it. I can tell you that such-and-such a person is dead and you know that, whatever else it means, it means the person is no longer here to be conversed with. Rising from the dead is of a quite different order and that is why it causes such difficulty for sceptics, whether believers or unbelievers. Unbelievers dismiss it as impossible or else as a religious myth of a dying and rising god. Sceptical believers find that they want to get away from a real, physical presence and to use 'resurrection' as a metaphor for spiritual and ethical rebirth. Here I affirm, as a doctrine of faith, that Christ is he who died and, behold, he lives.

What we celebrate, as the new fire blazes on this resurrection night, is not merely a remarkable rising from the dead, like Lazarus or the daughter of Jairus. We celebrate a definitive and permanent change in the relationship between life and death. Death is conquered by the Lord of life. As the third stanza of *Victimae paschali laudes* puts it: '*Mors et vita duello conflixere: dux vitae mortuus, regnat vivus*' (Death with life contended: combat strangely ended! Life's own Champion, slain, yet lives to reign). And every flame, every candle and every chant declares it – Christ is risen from the dead! Alleluia!

EASTER DAY
On the first day of the week

Early on the first Easter morning, when the sun, which had darkened over the cross, showed itself above the horizon, the three women, Mary of Magdala, Mary mother of James, and Salome, made their way to the tomb of Jesus in order to anoint his poor broken body (Mark 16.1–8). They went early in the hope that they would not be noticed, but they were prepared to take the risk because, having loved him in life, they continued in their desire to serve him in death.

These three women provide us with an example. What is striking about them is that they come before us, passing on their way to the tomb, with no expectation of reward. It is enough for them that they can do this humble service. Their greatest concern is the stone, and they wonder who will roll it away for them. As they approach they see, in amazement no doubt and with some fear of deception or foul play, that the stone, large as it is, has been rolled back. We can almost feel the tension as they advance toward the open tomb and, all three of them together, stoop and enter. And what they see – and what we too easily call an angel – is a young man in a white robe sitting at the right hand side. They see him and they are alarmed, and who wouldn't be? They did not expect to find a living being there.

The young man was undoubtedly an angel, for an angel is a messenger of God and this young man has an important message to deliver. The angel sits to the right because, according to the symbolism of right and left, the left represents the present life and the right eternal life. As Christ has already passed beyond the corruption of this present life and cannot die again, the angel sits at the right and is clothed in the white robe that proclaims the joy of a festival day. For the same reason the best vestments, gold or white, are worn on Easter Day. The angel's presence also reminds us that the festival of Easter belongs both to mortals and to angels, for the Redeemer's resurrection leads us children of Adam and Eve back to immortality, and the angels of God rejoice at our restoration.

The angel swiftly attempted to calm the frightened women, urging them not to be alarmed. He is very careful as he delivers his message. He identifies Jesus as being 'of Nazareth', to avoid any confusion, and adds 'who was crucified', showing that he knows who Jesus is and that he was dead. If this was an ordinary conversation between the women and some man having responsibility for the tombs, he might have said 'You are looking in the wrong place; his is the third tomb along in row five' or else explained that there was a mistake, a confusion, the body had been removed and laid elsewhere by order of the governor or of the chief priests. This message is not about cemetery plans or political machinations. The message is totally unexpected: 'He has been raised; he is not here.' He is not dead. He is not here.

And the angel has more to say: 'Go and tell his disciples and Peter that he is now going to Galilee; he will see them there just as he said.' Why the disciples *and* Peter? Simply because without this specific invitation Peter would not have gone with the disciples. How could he when he had three times denied that he was a disciple? Peter was called by name so that he would not lose hope and so that he would learn from his own weakness the virtue of mercy and the strength that comes from weakness.

The message is complete. The women emerged from the tomb and fled. Terror and amazement overwhelmed them. The message they had been given was not at first delivered, for here was an event that filled them with fear – the crucified teacher, laid in the tomb, was not dead. Joy would come to them, but on the first Easter morning they could not understand what had been told to them. It made no sense.

MONDAY OF THE FIRST WEEK
OF EASTER
Alleluia! Christ is risen

In the days to come we will see how the disciples gradually awakened to the joyful news and knowingly encountered the risen Lord. The cry that goes up from the Church is one of faith and the nature of faith is at the heart of our thinking about Easter. The women found the tomb empty and the body gone. As Jesus reveals himself to the disciples it is clear that his body, though able to pass through closed doors, bears the marks of nails and spear. This body can be touched and Jesus is able to break bread, to eat, to fish and to make a fire. Sceptics do not see how this can be and seek for other explanations. Before going on, I want to look at what it means if we live by faith.

Faith is initially 'faith in' someone; in our case it is faith in God, affirming that we are creatures and that the universe, in all the wondrous diversity that science identifies and maps, is the product of God's overflowing love. Faith begins with the affirmation 'I believe in God' but it goes beyond the statement to pour itself out in thanksgiving, praise and worship. To be Christian is to live confidently in the knowledge of the existence of God, source of life and love.

We know that faith does not suspend the changing nature of the world and that the love of God that sustains and defends us cannot, without violation of the created order, defend us from all harm. Faith enables us to live confidently, knowing that God will sustain us but reminding us as well, against the prevailing temper of the times, that death is not necessarily loss. We live confidently even in the face of death. To be 'faith', belief needs another element; that element is trust. I believe in God and I trust in God and in this faith I can advance. And faith, though not itself unreasonable, sometimes goes beyond reason. Christianity is not unreasonable, not absurd. It has an inner logic and coherence, but the key to it is faith. At the heart of Christianity is a mystery, a sublime incomprehensibility – the Creator as contemplated by the creature. I do not mean that we cannot think about it, discuss it, write about it, preach about it, but rather that it is never exhausted by our thought, never thoroughly understood, never comprehended.

What are we to do when life challenges us, when it seems that anything can happen and we have no control of it, when we fear the present and for the future? In such a situation we may hear Jesus castigate the disciples in the boat during the storm, calling them 'ye of little faith' and know that our faith too is weak. The Lord shows us our lack of faith, calls us to talk with him in prayer, to discuss everything with him, to entrust it to him. Now that is hard: that surrender to God; that openness to the will of God; that confidence that says 'Thy will be done' and gives up real action to God. 'Whenever I entrusted the matter completely to him,' wrote the spiritual guide Abbess Cécile Bruyère, 'without entering into all the reasonable considerations and legitimate fears, everything sorted itself out in the required time. So much so, that it was not long before I realised that the result depended upon my greater or lesser serene and blind confidence.'

The history of our faith shows that God clearly entrusts us who are Christians – who pray, who believe, who form together a worshipping community – with a task, with a number of tasks. Obstacles inevitably present themselves; they even accumulate. Should we leave the struggle, appealing to the name of 'impossibility'? No, for the impossible is the very region of faith, the point at which we pass beyond reason. As long as we move in the realm of the possible, we are only half sailing in the waters of grace, but when we leave the shore, when we launch out into the deep, when we entrust ourselves to God and go for that which seems impossible but which is clearly demanded of us, then faith takes us onward and God carries out marvels. This is the meaning of faith – and if we live by faith we live in the clear confidence that nothing is impossible to God. How could we think otherwise when our greatest cry of triumph is: Alleluia! Christ is risen.

TUESDAY OF THE FIRST WEEK OF EASTER
Out of the closed tomb

We know about God because God has chosen to reveal the divine nature to us and in doing so has chosen means which allow us to know God and to love God. In other words, God has chosen appropriate means in the same way that a teacher chooses the language and methods appropriate to a given age range and intellectual capacity. If we were simply faced with something utterly incomprehensible we would turn away bemused, as the women ran from the tomb. God has a purpose and that purpose is that we should be restored to eternal life. The means are not some brilliant angelic messenger but Jesus of Nazareth, the anointed one of God, who took our human nature and dwelt among us.

Certain aspects of his life and death go beyond our use of reason. We call these aspects 'miraculous'. Pope Gregory the Great, the last of the fathers of the Church, called such aspects 'wonderful' and in discussing them he favoured the sort of pairing of events that we find in the earlier fathers. The parallel between the sealed womb and the sealed tomb is found in John Chrysostom's homilies two hundred years previously. Gregory says:

The Lord's body which made its entrance to the disciples through closed doors was the same as that which issued before the eyes of men from the Virgin's closed womb at his birth. Is it surprising if he who was now going to live for ever made his entrance through closed doors after his resurrection, who on his coming in order to die made his appearance from the unopened womb of a virgin?

No, it is not surprising at all, nor is it surprising that those who doubt the bodily resurrection also doubt the virginal conception and birth. Personally I doubt neither but I can understand why people should. The Gospels are at pains precisely because of such doubts to demonstrate that the tomb was empty and to present the apparent contradiction between a body that passes through closed doors but can also be touched. What is, I suppose, surprising is that critics of Christianity are so lacking in imagination when what was unimaginable fifty or even twenty years ago is now normative – I mean microchips, virtual reality and the Internet.

The resurrection of Christ is linked to and is the precursor of the promise of our own resurrection. The apostle Paul tells us that our body will be 'like unto his glorious body'. Jesus, when he appears to the disciples, sees their faith wavering, so he greets them with words of peace, and shows them his hands and his side. He offered them the body which he brought in through closed doors so that they could touch it. In doing so he presented them with two things that are contradictory to reason, combining what is incorruptible with what can be touched.

For Gregory this was an important point. He was not a man in good health. He often told his congregation of his ailments. One Easter morning he told them he would preach despite his very sore throat! He was disappointed by the failings of his body, by sickness, by the corruptibility of the flesh. He had a strong interest in the incorruptible body. The material body could be touched and was corruptible. The spiritual, the immaterial, the content of godly dreams and visions was incorruptible and untouchable. In a wonderful and incomprehensible way, says Gregory, our Redeemer, after his resurrection, manifested a body that was incorruptible and touchable. By showing that it is incorruptible he would urge us on toward our reward, and by offering it as touchable he would dispose us towards faith.

WEDNESDAY OF THE FIRST WEEK
OF EASTER
The third day he rose again from the dead

Before we think further about resurrection and faith, I want
to look at the affirmation that we make when we say the
Apostles' Creed. First it says that the event took place 'on the
third day'. Christ's resurrection was not long delayed but
neither did it take place immediately after his death. If he had
returned to life immediately, there might have been some
doubt that he was really dead. If he had waited a long time
then it would have been less clear that he had vanquished
death and that this victory was for everyone. By waiting until
the third day the interval was sufficient to establish that he
was truly dead; to have gone longer may have meant that
hope was already fading – we see this in the words of
Cleopas addressing Jesus on the road to Emmaus: 'But we had
hoped,' he says, indicating loss of hope. 'But we had hoped
that he was the one to redeem Israel.' 'The third day' does
not, however, mean that Jesus remained dead for three full
days. In Matthew 12.40 Jesus says: 'For as Jonah was three days
and three nights in the belly of the whale, so will the Son of
Man be three days and three nights in the heart of the earth.'
This, however, seems to be a figure of speech in which a part
is taken for a whole. In the account of creation Genesis says
that the evening and the morning were one day, and that is
the way in which the Jews reckoned time, from evening to
evening, not from midnight to midnight. So, he died on the
sixth day, Friday by our reckoning, and was laid in the tomb
on that day. That is the first day. He remained in the tomb for

the whole of the sabbath, being the seventh day. That is the second day, ending at evening. And he rose from the dead on the third day, at midnight, if we follow St Gregory the Great, or at dawn, if we follow St Augustine of Hippo.

It says, second, that he rose again. It does not say 'on the third day he was raised' but 'he rose'. Jesus certainly raised others from the dead: one need only think of Jairus's daughter or of his friend Lazarus. Nevertheless, being raised from the dead is exceptional – there are very few cases of it in Scripture – and raising oneself never happens, except with Christ. Christ himself now rises. Sometimes it is said, as in Acts 2, that God raised him, and at other times that he arose. These two statements do not contradict each other because the divine power of the Father is identical with that of the Son and of the Holy Spirit. The resurrection is the work of God the Holy Trinity. Jesus had already spoken of this power when he said of his own life, 'No one takes it from me, but I lay it down of my own accord. I have power to lay it down, and I have power to take it again.' And again in John he tells the Jews 'Destroy this temple, and in three days I will raise it up' – and the evangelist, when he hears the Jews say that it took 46 years to build the Temple, adds this commentary: 'he spoke of the temple of his body'. Jesus, therefore, has this God-given power of offering up his life and taking it back again.

Third, it says 'from the dead'. The Revelation calls him 'the first-born of the dead'. Paul calls him 'the first-fruits of those who have fallen asleep'. Again we see that Jesus' resurrection is of a quite different order from previous resurrections or, as we might call them, resuscitations, for those who were previously restored to life were on borrowed time and would die again. Christ's is a perfect resurrection in that he is raised to an immortal life and is no longer subject to the necessity of dying.

This is not merely a statement about Jesus. It is a statement that leads on to our understanding that death is conquered and that through Christian faith and practice we come to share both in his death and in his resurrection. But a statement, especially one as short as this, cannot do justice to the mystery of resurrection. On Holy Saturday, as the new fire crackled and the flames shot upwards, as the column of wax became our sign of resurrection, as the faithful gathered and took their lights from the light that never fails, Christians experienced Easter and knew more of the gradual unfolding of the mystery and of the way in which it remains ultimately incomprehensible. In the liturgy rather than in theology we perceive the limits of understanding, the straining of language and the richness of signs. The Easter celebration is summed up in the Orthodox liturgy:

> Christ is risen, powerless are the demons.
> Christ is risen, the angels rejoice.
> Christ is risen, everywhere is the triumph of life.
> Christ is risen, there is no death more in the grave.

THURSDAY OF THE FIRST WEEK
OF EASTER
The resurrection of the dead

We now turn from Christ's resurrection to the affirmation in the Creed of our belief in our own resurrection. We find it referred to in Old Testament prophecy. The prophet Isaiah declared to Israel: 'Thy dead shall live, their bodies shall rise.' Ezekiel too prophesied that the graves would be opened and the dead raised and offered a wonderful account of what this resurrection might mean as the rattling bones hear the word of the Lord. This is a prophetic foretelling of the doctrine of the resurrection of the body that will be developed by the apostle Paul in the light of Christ's rising. If there is no resurrection, Paul argues, then Christ could not have been raised. Christ can be, and is, the first fruits of the resurrection of the dead, but he cannot be the unique example of resurrection. By his resurrection he introduces the possibility for us all of rising bodily from the dead. In 1 Corinthians Paul gives an account of what this will mean by showing us a mystery.

I have an active interest in the manner of resurrection because of the nature of the church in Smithfield where I am the Rector. It was founded in 1123 as a house of Augustinian Canons and though it lost its nave in 1539 the remarkable Norman quire remains, with its fine triforium gallery. The church has survived the Great Fire, Zeppelin raids and the Blitz. The founder, Prior Rahere, was buried in his church after his death on 20 September 1143. He was transferred to his present tomb on the north side of the sanctuary in 1405 and the Victorian antiquarians established that his bones are still there with his sandals on his feet. On the south side of the sanctuary stood the tomb of the founder of Emmanuel College, Cambridge, Sir Walter Mildmay, adorned with a large number of heraldic shields but no Christian symbols. During the nineteenth century it was moved to the south aisle and the coffins of Sir Walter and his wife were revealed in the process. They are still there. The church also has a large number of burials beneath the great stone slabs that form the floor.

Resurrection raises a number of quite specific questions for me. What will happen in the Priory Church at the resurrection? Will the Prior burst from his tomb? Will the Mildmay tomb be rent apart? Will the grave slabs be broken open as the dead rise? And what if the bodies are not intact? What if, for example, as at Chester Cathedral where they recently renewed the floor and carried out a survey of the under-floor burials, the introduction of gas, electricity or heating pipes had disturbed the remains, cutting through skeletons, rearranging or even losing bones or mixing them up? What of the ashes of my twentieth-century predecessors, Rector Sandwith and Rector Savage?

I believe these to be genuine questions, questions generated by the juxtaposition of biblical promise, doctrine and burial practice. We avoid these questions rather than answer them if we use the doctrine of the resurrection of the dead as a sort of parable for the rebirth of the soul or if we stress only the change from corruptible to incorruptible, from mortal to immortal. Jesus' rising involved his body, flesh and bones, organs, muscles and sinews. The flesh was incorrupt though marked by the nails, by the scourging and by his other sufferings, but the bones were unbroken, and nothing was lost. His resurrection came on the third day. The mortal remains we are concerned with here have been around much longer, a hundred years and more in most cases, over three hundred years for the Mildmays and more than 850 years for Prior Rahere. What do we believe will happen to them?

FRIDAY OF THE FIRST WEEK OF EASTER
And the life everlasting

A hundred years after Prior Rahere's death the debate about the resurrection was intense. If we read it today we are struck by its extreme literalism and materialism. Peter Lombard writing his standard textbook of theology, the *Sentences* – a manual that remained in use until the Reformation and which was to be found in Archbishop Cranmer's library – began by discussing the last trumpet call and then asked what age, height and sex the resurrected body would have. What, he enquired, would happen to those bits of us that had been discarded, hair and fingernails for example? His answers are fairly dull, and the Last Judgement seems to involve us having bodies that are pretty much like those we now have. Hugh of St Victor wondered whether we will be able to open and close our eyes in heaven. Honorius of Autun wondered what colour we would be in heaven and whether we would wear clothes. Several theologians wondered about the relation between our resurrected bodies and the food we had eaten, and this inevitably advanced to the question of cannibalism and who ended up with each bit. In the thirteenth century the discussion became a little less materialistic and dealt with the nature of the subtle body, a body like Jesus' risen body, that could disappear suddenly, pass through locked doors but also eat fish. Could we smell sweet odours or touch other bodies in heaven, they asked. Will we eat or taste? Eating seemed to be a particularly vexed question, for the indignities of digestion and excretion seemed inappropriate for the glorified body.

By contrast, the Muslim heaven is rich in bodily delights and eating involves neither digestion nor excrement. Perhaps the illustrations of the doctrine, paintings in churches, such as the Byzantine Last Judgement in the cathedral of Torcello, or Michelangelo's glorious east end of the Sistine Chapel, are easier to deal with. There we see the bones sorted out and gradually enfleshed, entering into their glorified state, or else deformed and grotesque, going to hell's gaping mouth.

Many of the questions posed by medieval theologians seem to us naive and unnecessary. We have tended to opt for the disembodied existence of the soul in preference to a worked-out doctrine of bodily resurrection. Yet modern science and especially developments in medicine present us with questions about our bodies and our selves that are not so very different from those asked in the Middle Ages. In our daily living we are not detached entities, body and soul, body and mind, but a single self. We are very much aware how the mind affects the body and the body the mind. The loss of memory and personality associated with Alzheimer's disease poses a difficult question about continuity in human identity. And issues raised by organ transplants, by developments in reproductive technol-ogy, and most recently by cloning, provide us with questions as straightforwardly materialistic as those asked by any medieval theologian. When is an organ part of a body and when isn't it? If we were to have transplants over a period of time of all the major organs, would we still be ourselves? What of the brain transplant or the whole-body transplant? Can I be regrown from genetic material preserved by freezing?

The question of resurrection and of what sort of body we will have has not become less complex or less material. Quite the contrary, we have, by scientific advance, reaffirmed the place of the material, the bodily, in human existence. It cannot be dispensed with. Resurrection, in its medieval guise, with a rattling of bones and the appearance of flesh on them, may seem both impossible and horrific. Theologians have tried other approaches which do not require the original material to be reused but which envisage the soul as a principle that must be embodied and which can shape matter into bodily form. That would give us new bodies, immortal, incorruptible, like unto Christ's own glorious body without the difficulties created by cannibalism or transplants. And yet the tradition is adamant about graves being opened, the sea giving up its dead, and all of that, and perhaps we cannot just discard it. After all, everything is possible to God, and our familiarity with the stories of the resurrection of Christ should not stop us seeing the amazement and bewilderment on the faces of the disciples. The dead are dead; we do not expect to meet them walking the streets. But here is one who was dead and is alive. That is the most amazing, bewildering, exciting thing, the culmination of the gospel, the heart of our faith. And if Christ be risen, which is what we affirm, then we too shall rise. Perhaps we need not worry too much about the details.

SATURDAY OF THE FIRST WEEK
OF EASTER
Known in the breaking of bread

The story of the road to Emmaus (Luke 24.13–35) is a familiar one and it presents us with precisely the sort of problems
about Jesus' risen body that have concerned us thus far.
Cleopas and his friend were talking of Jesus when they met
him. They were sorrowful, full of love for Jesus, but also full
of doubt when they heard that the women had found an
empty tomb and had a vision of angels. As they did not
believe in their hearts they could not see with their eyes. This
is not the first time in the Gospel that faith and sight have
been linked. The blind man with faith could see more clearly
than the religious leaders of the Jews who were blind to the
presence of Christ because they lacked faith. Sight without
faith is spiritual blindness. Jesus talked to the two disciples. He
admonished them for their foolishness, for their slowness in
believing the words of the prophets. He opened to them the
Scriptures, but they still lacked faith in him and so as they
approached Emmaus he made as if to go on. They had not yet
come to love him as the risen Lord but they were able to love
him as a stranger and they invited him to be their guest.
Actually, they did more than invite him. The Gospel text is
emphatic: they constrained him.

Gregory the Great preached on this passage and drew an
interesting conclusion from it. He saw that charity, love of
neighbour, love that conformed to the standard of the Christ,
who said 'Love one another as I have loved you', must be
more than an offer to be taken or left. Knowing that people,

from a sense of dignity and pride, may often refuse the charity they need, it must sometimes be offered with greater insistence, closer to compulsion or constraint. We must not be in the position of making an offer, hoping it will be refused, and glad when it is. 'Dearly beloved,' says Gregory, 'love hospitality, love works of charity.'

The meal at Emmaus was a moment of revelation. The disciples set the table and brought food, and Jesus, who was not recognized when he was speaking, deigned to be recognized, revealed himself, as he was being fed. At the table, as he sat at supper with them, he took bread and blessed it and broke it and gave it to them. What was it that opened their eyes? Was it perhaps that they had seen these hands do this same thing so many times, breaking the bread with which he fed the four and the five thousand, breaking bread in fellowship with his disciples countless times before he did it with the Twelve in the Upper Room on the night of his betrayal? In the moment of revelation he vanished from their sight, but so excited were they that they returned at once to Jerusalem, despite it being night. The Eleven told them that they had seen the Lord, and the two disciples told them all that had happened and how he was made known in the breaking of bread.

It is the experience of disciples today that Christ is still made known to us in the reading and exposition of Scripture and in the breaking of bread. He is made known when we are receptive to his revelation of himself. He does not force himself upon us but when we truly listen to the Word of God and diligently seek to know its meaning, rather than imposing upon it what we want it to say, we find the presence of Christ. And when we practise hospitality, receiving others at our table, and among them the stranger and not just our family and friends, Christ is present too. And when we extend open empty hands to receive the Body of Christ, the Bread of Heaven, so too is Christ present to us and given to us for food. Our Easter journey will find us frequently at meals with the risen Lord and will conclude when we give thanks for his Body and Blood in the Eucharist. The Emmaus story shows us that only faith provides the assistance to sight that will make the inward vision clear.

SUNDAY OF THE SECOND WEEK
OF EASTER
Mary stood beside the sepulchre weeping

There is surprisingly little weeping in the New Testament. There is weeping in the house of Jairus when his daughter died. The widowed mother escorting her son's bier weeps and is told by Jesus 'Do not weep.' There is much weeping over the death of Lazarus, over whom Jesus himself wept. And there is the woman who, at the Pharisee's house, stands behind him, at his feet – for he is reclining – weeping, and washes his feet with her tears, wipes them with her hair, kisses and anoints them. Peter wept when he realized that he had denied Jesus. The women of Jerusalem wept for Jesus and so did Mary of Magdala, standing beside the sepulchre.

The Magdalene may well not be, as Gregory the Great thought she was, the woman who wept over Jesus' feet and who was a sinner in the city, but Gregory is surely right when he says a great force of love burned within her and inflamed her. When the disciples who had come to look into the sepulchre and found it empty departed, she stayed. 'She sought for him whom she had not found, weeping as she searched; being inflamed with the fire of her love, she burned with desire for him whom she believed had been taken away. So it happened that she who stayed behind to seek him was the only one who saw him.'

Mary stood at the tomb and wept, but something impelled her to look in – though she knew the sepulchre was empty – and she saw two angels (John 20.11–18). They, who had every cause for joy, questioned her tears; she has no sooner answered them than she turns and, through tear-filled eyes, sees Jesus but does not know it is him. Her state is like that of the two disciples on the road to Emmaus. She did not yet believe that he was risen. 'Because she loved and doubted, she saw and did not recognise him. Her love revealed him to her, and her doubt prevented her from knowing him.' Jesus too asks why she is weeping. She was confused in her grief. She does not tell the person she imagines to be the gardener who it is she seeks. She says only 'If you have taken him away.'

It is perhaps one of the most moving moments in the Scriptures when Jesus addresses the weeping Mary, calling her by her own name, and as she heard him, and knew that she was herself known, she knew the one who called her. She replied to him, calling him 'Teacher'. All Mary's love was poured into that word, that recognition that he really was the one whom she loved, who, being dead, was alive. This new state, and the impending ascension, removes from Jesus and Mary that affectionate contact which may well have marked their love and friendship, but Mary now becomes the messenger and, as I have followed Gregory's thoughts about Mary, he must conclude them:

See, how the sin of the human race was removed where it began. In paradise a woman was the cause of death for a man; coming from the sepulchre a woman proclaimed life to men. Mary related the words of the one who restored her to life; Eve had related the words of the serpent who brought death. It is as if the Lord was telling the human race, not by words but by actions, 'Receive the draught of life from the hand of the one who offered you the drink of death.'

Presumably, Thomas the Twin had some basic rules – as we all have – for what he was willing to believe. Until Jesus' resurrection Thomas had been little more than a name on a list of the disciples. John does, however, record two of his utterances and these may help us to understand him a little better. The first came when Jesus was told that his friend Lazarus, the brother of Mary and Martha, was ill. Jesus waited for two days, until Lazarus was dead, and then told the disciples that he would go to Judea again. The disciples tried to stop him, reminding him that a very short time before the Jews had tried to stone him, but he is insistent that he must go. And not just him but the disciples as well. 'Let us go to him,' says Jesus. And Thomas said to his fellow disciples: 'Let us also go that we may die with him' (John 11.1–44).

Thomas is obviously totally committed to Jesus. He may not understand what is going on but he knows that he has become a disciple and he must follow the Rabbi wherever the Rabbi goes, even if that means death. So Thomas was there, standing at the entrance to the tomb when Jesus cried with a loud voice, 'Lazarus, come forth.' He saw the dead man come out, his hands and feet bound with strips of cloth, and perhaps he was among those who unbound him and set him free. What a marvellous thought that is. Did Thomas touch the body of Lazarus, the body that had been brought to death by sickness and had been in the tomb for four days, and if he did, what was it like? Did he touch his hands and his feet?

And did he then believe in Jesus, as some of the Jews did, because he saw this sign with his own eyes?

Thomas speaks again a little while after he has had his feet washed by Jesus at the Last Supper. Judas Iscariot has been identified as the betrayer. Peter has been told that he will deny Jesus that very night. The disciples are anxious; they quite suddenly feel that they have understood nothing. They do not know what is going on. Jesus tries to comfort them. 'Do not let your hearts be troubled,' he says. 'Believe in God, believe also in me' (John 14.1–7). And he tells them that they do in fact know the way to the place where he is going. Thomas pleads, 'Lord, we do not know where you are going. How can we know the way?' And Jesus replies: 'I am the way, the truth, and the life.' So here is Thomas again. He likes things to be clear cut. He likes to know the way. He wants things set out in front of him. Then, and only then, can he believe.

So we come to the appearance of Jesus to the disciples in the Upper Room after his resurrection – and Thomas isn't there. When the other disciples tell him 'We have seen the Lord' he says 'I will not believe' (John 20.24–9). 'If I can see the marks of the nails in his hands, if I can put my finger into the marks of the nails, and put my hand in the wound in his side, then I will believe.' Thomas wants evidence. He wants to be clear that it is not an hallucination, a vision, a ghost, a spirit.

TUESDAY OF THE SECOND WEEK
OF EASTER
See my hands and my feet

We can sympathize a good deal with Thomas. We too have difficulties about believing some things. Distant things matter very little. If we are told of the existence of some distant planet or moon, there is no reason for us to disbelieve. There is also no reason for us to seek definite confirmation. It has little effect upon us – unless we happen to be astronomers or cosmologists. But for immediate things – things that impinge upon us, that immediately affect us – it is different. We are told 'N is dead.' We say 'I can't believe it. I only saw him yesterday,' as if seeing someone yesterday is a guarantee that they continue to be alive today. Is not Thomas saying much the same thing: 'I can't believe it, for I saw him dead on Friday and it is only Sunday today'?

Notice that Thomas says 'I will not believe.' Believing involves the exercise of will, not of intellect. We do not believe because we have weighed up the evidence and found the matter reasonable. I am not suggesting here that our beliefs are somehow unreasonable, however. The key comes from another Thomas – the medieval theologian Thomas Aquinas. The will, he writes, plays the principal role in the knowledge of faith; the mind assents because of this impulse of the will and not because of evidence. We come to faith not through the accumulation of evidence but through reaching a turning-point, a moment of conversion after which we have a will to believe. And doubting Thomas could have believed if he would have.

The truth of this is demonstrated by the Lord's presence in his risen body. Jesus the Risen Saviour invites Thomas to touch him, to feel the holes, to put his hand into the wound in his side – and he will not. Without doing these things, he declares: 'My Lord and my God.' And Jesus then enunciates a fundamental principle on which Christianity operates: that of believing without seeing. It is not that we see the work of God and so we believe, but believing we see God at work in the world. Faith our outward sense befriending makes the inward vision clear.

'How do you come to believe?' a saintly man of God was once asked. And he replied, 'Go to church, behave in all things like a believer and you will come to believe.' Yet there is a place for questioning. Faith must seek understanding. In this faith, knowledge and love go together. Believing in Jesus we want to know more of him. Knowing him, we love him more. Loving him, we trust him more fully.

This Eastertide we greet the risen Lord with the words 'I will believe; though I do not now see you face to face or gaze upon your wounds or see the mark of the spear, yet I will believe.' And Jesus says 'Blessed are you.'

WEDNESDAY OF THE SECOND WEEK OF EASTER
My Lord and my God!

The name of Thomas the apostle is almost synonymous with scepticism, and 'doubting Thomas' has passed into English usage. Thomas does, however, perform a useful function. He shows, or at least his story shows, that the disciples were not credulous fools willing to believe anything. He also confers a certain legitimacy on our own doubts.

There are two areas of doubt in the resurrection narratives. The first concerns the identity of the Crucified One and the Risen One. There is that period between Good Friday and Easter morning which is hidden. Jesus is placed in the tomb and no one is able to see what happened in there. On the morning of the first day of the week the tomb is opened or found open and the corpse is gone. Then the appearances begin. Of course Jesus has to persuade and reassure the disciples. The dead do not suddenly rise from their tombs, not then and not now. Our first thought would be hallucination, that these visions are the product of a deep psychological desire for Jesus not to be dead. Our second, more hesitant, thought would be a ghost, whatever a ghost is, perhaps no more than a projection of an image. Jesus reassures the disciples, calls them by familiar names, performs familiar characteristic gestures, allows the wounds to be inspected, and eats and drinks. He does also disappear without trace and appears unhindered by locked doors. Nevertheless, and despite these differences, the New Testament is clear that the Risen One and the crucified Jesus are one and the same. Even Thomas, that model sceptic, is persuaded when he sees the marks of the nails and the pierced side, even if he doesn't touch them as he had first insisted he should do.

But there is another type of doubt. The disciples accepted the appearances of the crucified Jesus as of one risen from the dead. There remained a further question: was this the Christ, the promised Messiah? At an intellectual level this is the Christological question, the one that requires the sort of theological elucidation that will be provided, in due course, by Paul. At an urgent, existential level, this is the question of conversion, of seeing and believing and acting upon that belief, of turning the assent of the mind to assent of the heart, intellectual assent to real assent.

Without suppressing reason and the critical skills of the intellect, the New Testament shows that faith is a gift. We do not arrive at faith by a process of meticulous scholarly research, though that may quell our doubts. There is rather a point – the point of believing – when we make a step that goes beyond the evidence. Thomas made that step. It is not enough in that moment to say, 'Yes, I believe that you are the one who was crucified.' Thomas declares more boldly, 'My Lord and my God.'

It is faith, not knowledge, that is central to Christianity. We walk, it is said, by faith and not by sight. Faith, befriending our senses, our outward vision, makes the inward vision clear. Christianity is not irrational but reason does not exhaust the mystery. The mystery of redemption is accessible to faith and faith is that gift of God, that sublime working of the Spirit, freely available to us if, even with hesitation, with fear and trembling, with a list of unanswered questions, we receive it and trust God. 'Lord, I believe; help my unbelief.'

THURSDAY OF THE SECOND WEEK
OF EASTER
More about faith

There are two main ways in which the content of the faith is expressed in our worship – in formal statements and in praise. The Creed that we sing or say at the Eucharist every Sunday provides a formal statement of belief. If asked, 'Do you believe this?' then you could reply 'yes' or 'no' or say that you do not understand it. In other words the formal statement of the Christian faith is like any other sort of statement. The same rules apply. Language means the same within the church walls as it does outside those walls. I recognize, however, that there may be certain difficulties with propositional formulae, a problem that applies to all use of language. Assent can depend upon what each person under-stands by this or that statement.

The Creed contains a lengthy section that begins, 'And in one Lord Jesus Christ, the only-begotten Son of God.' It uses language that is not in general use. What does 'light of light' mean? Or 'Begotten not made'? What is here meant by 'substance'? How do we make sense of movement with regard to that place which is called heaven, from which Jesus appar-ently came down, and to which he subsequently ascended? Modern translations of the original Greek text agreed by the Council of Nicaea in 325 and revised by the Council of Constantinople in 381 cannot escape from the philosophical language of the time, merely substituting 'being' for 'substance'. But faith in Christ leading to salvation by divine grace does not depend upon knowledge. You do not need to know the

origin or the original text of the Nicene Creed. Even those
to be ordained are required only 'to believe the doctrine of
the Christian faith as the Church of England has received it'
and then to expound and preach it. Those who preach and
teach need to know how that doctrine was formulated, just as
the service staff of the garage need to know in considerable
detail how the car operates but, in order to drive it, you need
only to know what is necessary for the purpose – which does
not include knowledge of the workings of the internal
combustion engine.

This is, however, only one way in which doctrine is
expressed – explicitly and formally. It is also expressed implicitly and doxologically. 'Doxa' in Greek means 'praise'. Doxology
is praise put into words. The hymn 'Gloria in excelsis' is the
greatest example of Christian doxology. Its expressions of
praise, piled one upon another, have inspired generations of
composers: *Laudamus te, benedicimus te, adoramus te, glorificamus
te.* 'We praise thee, we bless thee, we worship thee, we glorify
thee.' Here too we find a large section devoted to Christ, but
whereas the section in the Creed is about Christ, the section
in the Gloria is addressed to Christ. Here is no carefully
thought-out statement of being and substance. Here Christ is
addressed by name and by title. Lord, only-begotten Son, Lord
God, Lamb of God, Son of the Father. And why? Because he
takes away the sins of the world and, sitting at the right
hand of the Father, is the source of mercy. Praise moves into
doctrine and the teaching about Christ leads directly, seam-
lessly, into petition before concluding again with a pile of
doxological superlatives: *quoniam tu solus Sanctus, tu solus
Dominus, tu solus Altissimus, Jesu Christe.*

It is easier to talk of the advantages and disadvantages of
monarchy in the seminar room than in the presence of the

monarch. It is much harder to criticize the monarchy when you have had the privilege of welcoming and speaking with the Queen. It is easier to talk theology in the classroom than it is in the church. It is much harder to criticize the structures and expressions of Christian faith and practice when you have welcomed Christ in word and sacraments. The experience of worship changes the perspective. It is not that it changes the function of propositional language; no, that remains the same. But the language of praise, the language of petition, is different; unconstrained, it leaps forward like the baby in Elizabeth's womb when Mary, pregnant with Jesus, came to visit her. Perhaps this is why the Church, a thousand years into her life, placed the Creed into the context of worship and bade us face the altar and address God as we affirm, *Credo in unum Deum*. Perhaps this is why we prefer to sing it, that the careful formulations of the Nicene fathers rendered into Cranmerian English might take wing and fly heavenwards, why we prefer to treat it as an affirmation of our faith and commitment rather than as an expression of its content.

The words cannot be divided. They form a coherent whole, doctrine and doxology mixing together, though doxology has priority, as faith seeks understanding. And we learn the content of faith by more than just these two texts – the prayers and the hymns also express it, implicitly, as the readings and the sermon make it explicit. Faith is never just about the proposition set down on paper requiring the signature of affirmation. Faith involves the totality of our being, all the levels and uses of our language, soaring on the wings of music, our minds in harmony with our voices.

FRIDAY OF THE SECOND WEEK
OF EASTER
Thomas the believer

We are concerned this week with faith, with the ability to say, without reservation or qualification, 'I believe.' One Holy Week, I read the sermons on the Apostles' Creed given by St Thomas Aquinas in Naples in 1273. The first sermon deals with the Creed as a whole or, as the Latin text says, 'Credo in unum Deum etc.' Aquinas begins by saying that the first thing necessary for any Christian is faith. Without faith, it is not possible to say that one is a Christian. People sometimes find this difficult. If I say of someone that he is not Christian, I am not impugning his behaviour, which may be of the sort that should distinguish Christians, for he may indeed love his neighbour as himself. No, I am simply stating that he does not believe the content of the Christian faith; that he is without faith, unless he has a faith known only to God.

Now Aquinas was well used to the opponents of faith and identifies their main objection as a claim that it is foolish to believe what is not seen. I like his four ripostes: First, he points to the imperfection of our intellect and the weakness of our knowledge. 'Our knowledge is weak to such a point,' he says, 'that no philosopher would be able to investigate perfectly the nature of a fly,' and tells of a philosopher who spent thirty years in solitude that he might know the nature of a bee! God is so far beyond our knowledge that it would be foolish to believe only what we can ascertain for ourselves. Second, Aquinas points to the levels of knowledge: a country bumpkin, a rustic, may dispute with a teacher, denying the truth of what is taught, but sensible people put the intellect of the teacher above that of the bumpkin. And the intellect of an angel is greater than that of the best philosopher and the divine intellect greater than all. Third, Aquinas addresses us right where we are, taking up the matter of faith and certitude. 'If everyone were willing to believe only those things that they might know with certitude, they would not be able to live in this world. How would anyone be able to live unless they put belief in someone? How would they even believe who their own father might be? And therefore it is necessary that human beings believe someone about those things which they cannot know perfectly by themselves.' Fourth, and finally, Aquinas weighs the argument that God proves to us that what faith teaches is true, for he sees the teachings of the saints as sealed, like a letter, with miraculous deeds that show forth God's power. The greatest miracle for him is that the world renounced the worship of idols and was converted to Christ by the preaching of simple men who were poor and few in number and who preached poverty and flight from the world's delights.

Of course the Angelic Doctor has not given us sure proofs because he does not believe in them. He believes that our vision is faulty and can be deceived but that the knowledge of God is never mistaken and that faith befriends our vision making clear what was hitherto hidden. His method is that of the fourteenth century, but the basic arguments do amount to a critique of knowledge and an argument that faith, in people if not in God, is necessary for living. I wonder if the ten disciples tried to argue Thomas out of his unbelief, reminding him of the miracles they had already seen performed, telling him that he should trust their collective witness, that they had seen the marks of the nails even if he hadn't. They didn't succeed and I find that arguments against unbelief rarely succeed – though I would maintain that we do have a duty to criticize the prevailing popular understanding of the nature of truth. It is, after all, extraordinary that people will believe uncritically a curious package of distorted eastern religions and reject without even a cursory examination the content and structure of Christian faith. Christianity does not eschew the use of the critical intellect in matters of religion but it does enter a caveat against reason as a sure guide in the things of God.

Some people will be persuaded and the apologetic task is more necessary today than ever before but I still hold that it is worship, that it is the palpable presence of God in our liturgy, that encourages and enables the step from vague belief in a spiritual undergirding to our existence to explicit belief in God. It is because Christ, crucified and risen, is to be found in the liturgy, because he is made present by the consecratory rite, and says to all who will listen 'Do not doubt but believe.'

Two Thomases – Thomas the doubter, Thomas the believer – but doubting Thomas moved from radical unbelief and a demand for proof to a profession of faith that went beyond anything uttered by those who had already seen the Lord, and Thomas the great theologian moved from confidence in the human intellect to simple contemplation of the divine mystery, a contemplation that is more prayer than theology. The Church needs its theologians, and especially theologians who believe passionately but not uncritically, but it also needs those who pray, worship, adore and contemplate the mystery of God's love for us.

SATURDAY OF THE SECOND WEEK
OF EASTER
Wholehearted fidelity to God

At the beginning of the First Week of Easter I asked what it means to live by faith and defined it in this way: To be Christian is to live confidently in the knowledge of the existence of God, source of life and love. Now that we have looked at the two Thomases and their attitudes to faith, I want to carry on with this investigation and to keep Abbess Cécile as our guide. First, however, let me tell you something about her. She was born in Paris on 12 October 1845, and named Jenny. In the spring of 1857 she was prepared for her first communion by the founder of the Abbey of Solesmes, Dom Prosper Guéranger. At that point there began a deep harmony between them, though the Abbot was forty years older; it lasted until his death. 'I have never raised a question with this child,' he said, 'without realizing that the Holy Spirit has been there before me. It is like playing the piano; when one strikes, she resonates.' Another abbess, Dame Gertrude d'Aurilac Dubois, of Stanbrook at the foot of the Malvern Hills, would come to admire 'the wisdom and simplicity which seemed to play within and around her, strength and sweetness, activity and unshakeable peace, extraordinary intuition and childlike grace.' Cécile, as she was called in religion, was to be, at 22, prioress of the new foundation for Benedictine nuns at Solesmes and was named abbess at 27. She presided over her abbey until her death in 1909 at the age of 63; she died at St Cecilia's Abbey in Ryde on the Isle of Wight, where her community had gone into exile in 1901 because of anti-religious laws.

Now let us turn to her teaching, and in particular her teaching on serenity and joy. 'The measure of our faith,' she wrote, 'is the measure of our joy.' 'Do you want to praise God?' she asks, 'then be resolutely joyful in the midst of everything, so that the atmosphere of joy becomes a habit, the ordinary impetus of the soul, and that not because things are necessarily pleasant but because it is God who sends them.' As I previously observed, we know that faith does not suspend the changing nature of the world and that the love of God that sustains and defends us cannot, without violation of the created order, defend us from all harm. Faith enables us to live confidently, knowing that God will sustain us but reminding us as well, against the prevailing temper of the times, that death is not necessarily loss. We live confidently even in the face of death. Abbess Cécile takes us a step further, showing us that joy is the manifestation of that confidence.

The habit of joy leads to serenity. God is the source of all blessing, all beatitude, all joy. We cannot enter into contact with him in adoration or prayer, in worship or the sacraments, without peace, calm, serenity and joy flooding the soul – that is, if we do not present obstacles to that flood. To maintain, therefore, this sense of serenity, this inner joy, we must stay close to God. Abbess Cécile says, 'Serenity is a barometer which directs you accurately enabling you to gauge whether, through all the ups and downs of life, you are faithful in most perfect love.' This interior serenity involves an act of will. We are responsible beings. We are not just to be driven this way and that; it requires action on our part. It requires putting God first, ordering and reordering our lives so that they are based on faith, on wholehearted fidelity to God.

Serenity overcomes self-love, pride and ill-regulated passions; what the Prayer Book calls 'unruly wills and affections'.

Serenity gives God complete sway over the soul; this isn't possible when we are in a constant state of agitation, even if what agitates us is good in itself. Serenity preserves right judgement – with it the eye of the soul, outward vision aided by faith, is continuously clear, whereas agitation stirs up so much dust that we cannot see the truth. Serenity prevents the light of faith from flickering, and it enables us in loving God steadfastly to love and serve our neighbours also.

Abbess Cécile was a Benedictine, and one of the marks of the Order, something that comes directly from the Rule of St Benedict, is realism and with it an understanding of human imperfection, especially of those failings that arise by surprise or awkwardness. Imperfection, willing or unwilling, is to be regretted, but it is to be corrected in the same way that the supple branch springs back into place when no longer pressed down by some weight. It requires a return to fidelity and not guilt-ridden self-abasement. Serenity makes us strong, magnanimous and persevering. After the examination of our imperfections in Lent, Eastertide is a season for greater faithfulness, greater serenity, and above all for greater joy.

SUNDAY OF THE THIRD WEEK
OF EASTER
The Lamb's high banquet

Jan van Eyck's altarpiece for the Church of St Bavo in Ghent
was completed in 1432. Something over 17 feet long when
opened and 12 feet tall, it expresses a profound spiritual
understanding of the economy of human salvation, taking us
in translucent images from Adam to apocalypse, from Eve
into eternity. When closed, the images speak of promise, of
what is as yet unfulfilled. In the upper register, prophets and
sibyls announce the coming of the Messiah. Beneath them
Gabriel with iridescent wings addresses his greeting to Mary.
The Virgin's reply is written upside-down for it is to be read
by God in heaven. At the lowest level, the patrons flank two
statues painted onto the altarpiece, the two St Johns – the
Baptist, holding the Lamb of God, and the Divine, writer of
the Revelation, who gave the Lamb central place in his
description of the heavenly scene.

Inside, the altarpiece has two levels. At the centre of the
higher level, hand raised in benediction and crowned with
power, is God the Father. At his right hand, Mary, now in
splendid robes and wearing a crown. At his left hand, John
the Baptist. These two are pre-Christians, forerunners, active
collaborators in the work of salvation, who believed the
promises of God. Each of the saints is flanked by charming
angelic musicians, singers and instrumentalists. At the outer
edges, clutching fig leaves, are Adam and Eve. Eve, naked,
with her fig leaf providing scant cover, holds a rather ugly
looking little fruit, hardly worth disobedience. It is a visual
joke – Van Eyck has placed in Eve's hand an orange of an

unusual sort, having a thick, roughly textured pale yellow skin; it is called 'Pomum Adami' – Adam's apple!

The scene in the lower tier runs the full 17 feet of the altarpiece. It is crowded, like so many scenes of adoration, with angels, apostles, virgins, prophets, patriarchs, martyrs, matrons, confessors, holy hermits and pilgrims, and at the centre of it all, atop an altar that could have been borrowed from any decent church, complete with altar cloth, frontal and superfrontal, is the Lamb of God, the Christ. In a series of connected images, though not a narrative, Van Eyck links the sin of Eve and Adam, through prophetic utterances, to the annunciation to Mary and John's call to repentance. He sums up the redemptive work of Christ in the image of the Lamb that takes away the sins of the world.

Eve in her nakedness and God the Father in robes of imperial splendour are familiar images, as are the bishops in their copes and mitres and the warriors on their chargers, but this lamb, standing uncomfortably on the altar and being censed by thurible-swinging angels, is so incongruous, so unexpected, so amazing, that it reverses and negates all expectations and turns upside-down all ordinary perceptions of power and success. Here is the lamb, the sacrificial creature taken from the flock, unaware of its fate, bleating pathetically; it is not a likely symbol for power, quite unlike the soaring eagle or the roaring lion. Yet it is the lamb who has triumphed, the lamb who is worshipped, the lamb who establishes it as a divine principle that the one who puts down the mighty from their seats and exalts the humble and meek also justifies the innocent. We are faced again with the discomfort that comes to mortals when they contemplate the divine, a discomfort which finds no solution until our struggling thoughts give way to worship and we are lost, to ourselves but not to God, in wonder, love and praise.

MONDAY OF THE THIRD WEEK
OF EASTER
Christ our Paschal Lamb

We need to think some more about Christ's victory over sin and death, and I want to look at it using the tool we have been given, the images of Jesus as the lamb and as the shepherd. There is really a great gulf fixed between sheep and shepherd – the distance between animal and human. No matter how much we may love an animal, even a really responsive cat or dog, animals remain more unlike us than like us. One day at a theme park with a children's farm I watched one of the keepers petting a ram. It looked like a really affectionate encounter on both sides. But she said that he was only interested in the contents of her bucket, apples and carrots and similar things. The words from the Book of the Revelation to John must therefore be judged as at best paradoxical and at worst nonsensical. 'The Lamb at the centre of the throne will be their shepherd.' This is what the angel tells John. The Lamb will be a shepherd. Now if I said to you: 'The lamb will drive you home', you would surely tell me that this is absurd as lambs cannot drive. If I tell you that the shepherd will drive you home, that will sound quite reasonable. Yet we accept quite easily the statement in the Revelation as we also accept in the Eucharist the statement concerning the consecrated bread, 'This is the Lamb of God.'

We are therefore dealing with figurative language rich in imagery, language that presents us with a paradox no less profound. The sheep and the shepherd are different, but the distance between Creator and creature, between God and humankind, is greater still. Jesus, the good shepherd, knows his sheep because of this astonishing degree of identification with them. The Lamb becomes the shepherd. The Lamb, who has known death, and now knows glory, is able to be the shepherd. And God becomes Man, and sharing our human life and death, and knowing pain before coming to joy, and crucifixion before coming to glory, is perfectly identified with us so that we may be identified with him.

The images are here laid one over the other as if by some clever special effect, some trick of film or television. Language fails us at this point. We sense that. We recognize that much of the language of Scripture and liturgy, though it conveys truth, is simply not literal. Here the Lamb may be a shepherd, even if sheep can't drive cars! Here bread becomes Christ's body. Here wine becomes his blood. Here in the water of baptism and in Holy Communion we are so closely united with Christ that we carry his name. And we know that language often fails – that the poet, the artist, the musician will express feeling with much greater facility than ordinary words will allow and with greater truth.

Jesus says: 'My sheep hear my voice. I know them, and they follow me. I give them eternal life, and they will never perish.' Do we really need to unpack this or can we affirm clearly that this is the meaning of Easter? We are given eternal life. We will never know what it is to perish.

TUESDAY OF THE THIRD WEEK
OF EASTER
The Lord is my shepherd

The most frequent landmarks of the *Campagna*, the country-side around Rome, other than the conspicuous towers, relics of the feuds between the great Roman families, Frangipani, the Orsini and the Colonna, are the conical huts, refuges for the shepherds. This may not be true today but it was at the beginning of the twentieth century when that professional tourist and guidebook writer Augustus Hare compiled his charming book *Days near Rome*. Also to be found were round huts built of reeds and rifled tombs that were sometimes used as houses. The poet Virgil saw them in the days of ancient Rome and little had changed in nearly two thousand years. The shepherds lived in those houses for about half the year and were cut off from all social and civilizing influences. They wore broad-brimmed hats, long, loose jackets made of unshorn sheep- or goatskin, and leggings. The smoke of their fires escaped from the open apex of their conical huts, which slept several people as well as large white dogs and pigs. Sometimes the sheep and the goats also enjoyed the warmth and shelter. It is with such a context in mind that we should hear Jesus say 'I am the good shepherd.' The shepherd lived, until very recently, on the margins of society, separated by force of circumstance, and those likely to be shepherds were those who had no better place or work. It was the prodigal, the outcast, the hireling, who found employment with the flocks. Shepherds were rough, unlettered people. They did not make good witnesses. That makes the angelic announcement of Christ's birth, to them before all others, remarkable.

We see already in that act the entry of Jesus into the margins of society. It was perhaps because of this that the early Christians found in the good shepherd one of the most reassuring images of the Lord (one that we will explore more thoroughly tomorrow). As the good shepherd Jesus is not the lord and the judge but one who understands poverty and rejection, one who is constant in love, and is a companion even in the valley of the shadow of death. The image of the good shepherd disappears after AD 400 but it reappeared with dramatic power in Anglican devotion. Perhaps it springs from a rather idyllic view of the countryside (one that can hardly be maintained after BSE and foot-and-mouth), or perhaps it spoke to our Victorian and Edwardian forebears of a simpler life. Whatever the case, Christ the Good Shepherd looked down on many Sunday school rooms in the 1950s. 'The King of love my shepherd is', together with 'The Lord's my shepherd', sung to Crimond, remain firm favourites, the latter especially as we commend the departed souls to God's care and ask that they may be known as 'sheep of thine own flock, souls of thine own redeeming'.

The comfort this brings is important; there are times when we need it, and the contemporary Church, wary of being or becoming comfortable, has stressed discomfort too much. Yet the image of Christ as a good shepherd, laying down his life for the sheep, as well as the one who seeks out the lost and the straggler, is packed with meaning and operates at many levels. We must not simply choose the most comfortable. It calls us to examine the ways in which the good news reaches the margins of our society and those other sheep that will be united to the one flock, under the one shepherd.

WEDNESDAY OF THE THIRD WEEK
OF EASTER
I am the good shepherd

The good shepherd, then, is one of the most beautiful and evocative images in the Gospels. It was an image that translated readily into art such that one of the earliest symbolic depictions of Christ is a late third- or early fourth-century statue, in the Vatican Museums, of a young beardless shepherd in a short belted tunic, carrying a satchel and with a ram firmly held on his shoulders. You may have seen another slightly younger version, from the fourth century, in the 'Seeing Salvation' exhibition at the National Gallery during the millennial year 2000.

It stands at the end of a long progression of images drawn from life among the herds. The patriarchs of Israel were herdsmen. We find Abraham and Lot going together with their flocks and parting because their herdsmen quarrelled. We find Jacob, whom God called Israel, meeting Rachel when she brings her sheep to the well. Joseph goes out to seek his brothers in the pastures and is waylaid by them and sent into slavery in Egypt. Moses tends the flocks of his father-in-law Jethro on the slopes of Sinai and there encounters the God of the burning bush. The contrast between the values of the shepherd in the fields and of the dwellers in towns features in the story of David the shepherd-boy and of King Saul. Psalm 23 relates God's care for his people to the affirmation that 'The Lord is my shepherd' and Ezekiel prophesies against the shepherds of Israel, that is to say the political and religious leaders, who feed themselves rather than the sheep, who do not bring back the strayed or seek out the lost. 'I myself will be the shepherd of my sheep,' says the Lord God. 'I will seek the lost, and I will bring back the strayed, and I will bind up the crippled, and I will strengthen the weak, and the fat and the strong I will watch over. I will feed them with justice.' I have to draw the conclusion from Ezekiel 34 that the equivalent of our 'fat cats' was 'fat sheep'. The ideas found here are carried over into the parable of the lost sheep in Luke 15 and in this 'I am' saying of John: 'I am the good shepherd' – that is to say, the fulfilment of prophecy.

It is a beautiful and evocative image but it does not translate easily into theology. Both John Chrysostom, Bishop of Constantinople, in the fifth century, and Pope Gregory the Great in the sixth preached on this Gospel. Chrysostom first of all relates it to the task of presiding over the Church, to the bishop as pastor and shepherd, showing that Christ did not change his attitude or his teaching when threatened with death but stood firm and chose to accept death rather than betray his mission. 'I lay down my life,' says Jesus, and in that way shows that he is not a charlatan or a deceiver but is a true witness. Chrysostom is perhaps thinking here of those who claimed to hold the Christian faith but who apostatized in the face of persecution. Finally he notes, as all commentators do, that the sheep whom the good shepherd tends are not just those of Israel but that 'other sheep' is here taken to mean the Gentiles.

Gregory was a less intellectual preacher than John Chrysostom, and more practical, but his message was essentially the same. Jesus calls himself the good shepherd and defines the character of goodness in terms of a willingness to lay down his life for the sheep. The way we are to follow is, therefore, one that stands in contempt of death. One must, says Gregory, give of all that one has, that is to say goods and possessions, for the well-being of the flock, and then one's life as well. This sitting light to worldly goods is a preparation for sitting light to life itself. That person is a hireling or hired hand who holds the place of shepherd but does not seek the profit of souls. He is eager for earthly advantages, rejoices in the honour of preferment, feeds on temporal gain, and enjoys the deference offered him by other people. This is his reward.

But Gregory goes further – we cannot know whether anyone is a shepherd or a hireling if there is no occasion to test him. And Gregory is not talking here of apostasy or of flight. His message is much more relevant for us when we consider ourselves or others as leaders worthy of honour. When the flock of Christ is assailed in any way, by injustice, by fanaticism, by teaching that is not conformable to the Scriptures, then

> the one who appeared to be a shepherd, and was not, leaves the sheep and flees . . . He does not flee by changing his place but by withholding his help; he flees because he sees this unrighteousness and is silent; he flees who conceals himself beneath his silence.

Because the hireling esteems honour, because he enjoys temporal advantages, he is, says Gregory, afraid to oppose the danger lest he loses what he loves.

Gregory has pondered the human heart. He knows how attracted we may be to what we have and unwilling to risk it, even for righteousness' sake. His astute observations reveal the danger he himself is in – he knows this – and that of religious and political leaders at every level, and everyone, every one of us who values office, title, fame, honour, reputation, wealth, position, status. Let no seductive good fortune lead us astray. We are called by the good shepherd to be ourselves good shepherds caring, in whatever situation we find ourselves, for those committed in any way to our charge. It is a foolish traveller, he says, who sees pleasant meadows on his journey and forgets where he is going.

THURSDAY OF THE THIRD WEEK
OF EASTER
Children, have you any fish?

Have you anything to eat? These are the words of Jesus to his disciples as recorded by St Luke. This is one of two incidents recorded in the Gospels in which Jesus eats with them after his resurrection. The other is recorded by St John and it tells of Jesus preparing breakfast on the shore of the Sea of Galilee on a fire of coals that had fish laid on it and bread. Jesus asked them to bring the fish they had brought and said to them 'Come and eat.'

We have already heard from the Gospel homilies of Pope Gregory the Great. Born around 540, Gregory became Bishop of Rome in 590 and died in 604. He came from a noble family but sold his estates, devoting the money to the relief of poverty, and entered a monastery, where he lived a very austere life. He gave it up under protest when made one of the seven deacons of Rome. He was a man who combined deep faith with practical sense, his firmness and strength of character were tempered by gentleness and charity and he was able to overcome many of the political and ecclesiastical difficulties that faced him when, after a severe interior struggle, he became Pope. He was extraordinarily busy, resolving political conflicts, stopping the crumbling fabric of the city of Rome collapsing, writing, preaching, founding and reforming monasteries, promoting church music, and all this in spite of recurrent ill-health. So I looked to him again to provide some unique insight into this reading, and of course he did, albeit rather obliquely.

Gregory's sermon on the story from John refers to the story in Luke. We do not have a sermon of his on the Lucan story, and the paragraph that we do have suggests that the version of Scripture that he had was just a little different from what we have. According to Gregory, when Jesus asked his disciples 'Have you anything to eat?' they gave him broiled fish and some honeycomb which he ate with the fish. We must remember that the text of the Bible has been copied and translated countless times and that we have the benefit of translations made by careful comparison with the most ancient manuscripts, manuscripts that were unknown in sixth-century Rome. And when I looked in my Greek New Testament there was the alternative reading that said that the disciples gave Jesus not only part of a broiled fish but also some honeycomb; this alternative reading is attested by a number of authorities but not so many as to get it into our text. It is, however, precisely this reference to honeycomb that appealed to Gregory.

Twice, says Gregory, Jesus eats broiled fish and – this is a crucial point in early biblical interpretation – no action that is repeated is without a mystical meaning. To broil means to burn or more specifically to cook by placing on the fire or on a gridiron over it, to make very hot. It is, incidentally, the same root from which we get *brulée*. What then do we believe that the broiled fish signifies? Gregory is clear – it signifies Christ the mediator between God and man who suffered. Now that is a big jump for us, for our minds are more literal in their interpretation and less mystical. We know that the fish is an early symbol of Jesus, for the Greek word for fish, *ichthus*, can be an acronym for Jesus Christ, Son of God. Gregory says:

he who condescended to conceal himself in the waters of the human race, wished to be caught in the net of our death, and he was broiled, so to speak, by turmoil at the time of his passion. But the one who condescended to be broiled like a fish in his passion became a honeycomb for us in his resurrection.

Jesus therefore intended, says Gregory, to show by this combination of honeycomb and broiled fish that those who here endure affliction for the sake of truth are to be received into the true delight of eternity by one who has already suffered for them.

FRIDAY OF THE THIRD WEEK
OF EASTER
Death hath no more dominion over him

Eastertide moves us inexorably towards the ascension of our
Lord and the gift of the Holy Spirit at Pentecost. But Friday
remains a day associated with the Passion and so I must inter-
rupt the flow of these meditations for a day and return to
Simon Peter tomorrow. During a brief visit to the Spanish
capital, Madrid, in 2000, I was able to visit the Thyssen
Museum and the Prado. It was Eastertide, but visiting these
galleries returned me to the Passion and particularly to Good
Friday night. I was drawn to images of the deposition: the
dead Christ being taken from the cross, carried in a great
winding cloth to the tomb, laid on a slab prior to burial. The
most powerful of these, by the Flemish artist Rogier van der
Weyden, has almost life-size figures of Christ, the Blessed
Virgin, St John, St Mary of Magdala and others. Painted 565
years ago, its colours are vibrant and the emotion displayed
there tangible. Without interference from gallery attendants
you can get so close to the painting that you can see clearly
the tears rolling down the cheeks of the beloved disciple as
he looks at Mary, his new mother, in a dead faint, with a pallor
if anything more death-like than that of her son. And the
wounds of Christ, the holes made by the nails, the gaping
bloody wound in his side, the trickle of blood from the points
where the thorns pierce his brow, are all so realistic that it is
painful to look on them and to contemplate Christ in his
agony. I cannot imagine what it must have been like to have
said Mass in front of this altarpiece day by day. In another

striking painting, by Antonello de Messina, a Sicilian who learned his art in Spanish Flanders before settling in Venice, a weeping angel, its face contorted by sorrow, like a lost child, embraces the dead Christ.

Perhaps it is a particular feature of Spanish spirituality, of the Spanish temperament, that there should be such realism in devotional art. The figure on the Spanish crucifix is generally dying or dead, and perhaps this seriousness in the face of dying is a counterpoint to the extravagance of Marian devotion and the elaborately vested Madonnas that adorn so many churches, to the great fiestas that mark major liturgical celebrations. Whatever the case I found myself not in the midst of Easter joy but back between the cross and the tomb, and was therefore the more readily struck by Bramantino's extraordinary painting of the risen Christ. It could so easily be a painting of the dead Christ. As with van der Weyden and Messina we have painful realism, blood, tears and anguish, we have death's pallid hue. But the eyes are open – bloodshot but open – and the eyes reveal confusion, surprise, that strange sense of being alive when one should be dead. Bramantino's Christ is not some rather insubstantial figure rising from the grave carrying a banner, but in truth one who was dead and is alive, one marked irrevocably by the experience of dying such that we find in Christ the risen Lord the fullness of human experience up to and including death. These artists have presented to us experience that goes beyond words and renders us silent. They underline the seriousness of the death Christ died and the truly miraculous and unexpected nature of the conquest of death.

I think we need to revisit the cross and the tomb, both sealed and empty, if our appreciation of resurrection is not to become divorced from the reality of death; if we are not to substitute the spiritual and even the mystical for the material reality. Christ appears to the disciples in that body that was crucified and which, though now much changed, by the process of death and resurrection, remains his embodiment. We are, like him, embodied beings: dwelling physically and concretely in a given space, at a given time, and this mortal life will end in a death and lead, by faith in Christ, to resurrection, to the life that we call eternal. But nothing in Christianity tells us to minimize the importance of death – not Christ's death, not our death – but to see that, Christ being raised from the dead, death hath no more dominion over us.

SATURDAY OF THE THIRD WEEK
OF EASTER
Tend my sheep

After breakfast with the Lord, the third occasion in John's Gospel that he had made himself known to the disciples after his resurrection, Jesus walks along the shore with Simon Peter. John tells us that when Jesus appeared on the shore and called out to them 'Children, have you any fish?' and then instructed them where they should lower their nets, 'the disciple whom Jesus loved' said 'It is the Lord!' Peter stripped off, sprang into the sea and swam to the shore. With breakfast concluded Jesus takes Peter aside, and asks him 'Simon, son of John, do you love me more than these?' What a dreadful question this is for Peter! A reproach might have been easier to bear. Peter's tongue has always been swift and ill controlled. He has declared his love before and become the one who denied Jesus. He does not ask Jesus the reason for the question; he replies very simply: 'Yes, Lord, you know that I love you. You know, Lord, that despite my headstrong foolishness, despite the denial I made, I do, I really do, love you and my love is greater than anyone else's love for you.' Jesus responds with a straightforward admonition: 'Feed my lambs.'

The process is repeated. Jesus asks the very same question. Peter gives the same answer. Jesus' reply is different: 'Tend my sheep.' And the process begins again. Peter is grieved by the third question and clearly uncertain as to how he can give Jesus the assurance he seeks. His reply is more emphatic: 'Lord, you know everything; you know that I love you.' Jesus charges him: 'Feed my sheep.' But the questioning is over and

Jesus goes on to tell Peter about what will happen to him. His language is veiled but the evangelist is certain that 'he said this to show by what death he was to glorify God'.

Peter the fisherman becomes Peter the shepherd, tending the flock of Christ, feeding both lambs and sheep. The Magnificat antiphon for first Vespers of the feast of Saints Peter and Paul declared Peter's new role:

> Thou art the shepherd of the sheep, O Prince of the Apostles; to thee have been given the keys of the kingdom of heaven.

And the hymn at Lauds called him *bone Pastor*, good and blessed Shepherd. He was the first, after Christ himself, to take on this role, and every shepherd since then has known that God does not choose us for ministry because of our strengths but because of our weaknesses. He does not eliminate those weaknesses, but they provide the space that is filled by his grace. Hence, and here I write most obviously as a priest, we can never boast of what we have done but are always aware that it is God who works in us. The glory belongs not to us but to him, and if there is failure – well, then we are reminded that God does not ask for success in ministry, but faithful adherence to Christ. Peter found himself cast into the very role that Jesus had defined, that of the good shepherd. He knew that he could never fill that role. He knew the extent of his failures and faults. Christ acting in and through his person remained – and remains – the true, the great, the good shepherd.

SUNDAY OF THE FOURTH WEEK
OF EASTER
O happy fault

In this fourth week the Sunday liturgy is beginning to think about Jesus' departure – 'A little while and you will see me no more, again a little while and you will see me' – but, taking our lead from the Van Eyck altarpiece, I want us to go back to the Easter vigil and to the lighting of the new fire and the Paschal Candle. The vigil and its readings, like the resurrection itself, was too much to take in all at once. There is a line in the blessing of the candle, that lengthy benediction known from its opening word as the Exsultet (*Exsultet jam Angelica turba caelorum*: 'Now let the host of angels rejoice'), which refers salvation back to Adam:

> O truly necessary sin of Adam, that Christ's death
> blotted out!
> O happy fault (*felix culpa*), that merited such
> a Redeemer!

It is not a line that has found much favour with the twentieth-century revisers of the liturgy. They cannot see how any fault can be a happy one or any sin necessary. The Exsultet moves close to a position in Jesus' own teaching about how it is the sick that need a physician and the sinful a redeemer, and in his stories of the lost sheep, the lost coin and the lost son. The finding of the sheep and the coin and the return of the prodigal son were sources of great rejoicing. There would have been less cause for joy if they had not first been lost.

This position is summarized in what Jesus says of the woman who anointed him, washing his feet with her tears: 'I tell you, her sins, which were many, have been forgiven; hence she has shown great love. But the one to whom little is forgiven, loves little' (Luke 7.47). A similar approach is found in St Paul when he saw that God's grace was sufficient to deal with any sin, and the greater the sin, the greater God's love for the sinner, the greater the divine mercy. Paul, however, had to go on to deny that sin should abound so that grace should abound the more. His reservations do not undermine the main point. When we sin, through ignorance, through weakness, even through our own deliberate fault, the grace of God is sufficient for us and that grace is intended to bring us back to friendship with God. Paul knew this from the bitter experience of being a persecutor of the Church and then being chosen by God to build up what he had once set out to destroy.

The Church read this teaching back into creation. We find it in the collect after the first vigil reading, which is the account of creation in Genesis 1, that points to how God wonderfully created us and yet more wonderfully restored us. It is a part of the logic of salvation which is not a part of our ordinary logic. Adam's sin, which created a debt to God the Father, is wiped out and the debt repaid by the shedding of Christ's dear blood. So great is the benefit of the redeeming act that the Exsultet counts life as nothing without it. The stain of sin afflicting all humankind revealed the fullness of divine mercy and compassion. 'How wonderful the condescension of thy mercy,' sings the deacon. 'How far beyond all reckoning thy loving kindness. To ransom thy slave, thou gavest up thy Son!' The vigil readings, which we will now consider, set out the history of that loving kindness, helping us to understand how Adam's sin could be thought of as necessary, how it could be the *felix culpa*.

Although it may confuse our logic, the idea of a *felix culpa* is part of our experience. We have all had the avoidable accident, the moral failure, that led to something so worthwhile that we are ultimately grateful for the fault that caused it. We cannot make it a principle that we should be sinful in the hope of such an outpouring of grace, but the fact that it happens shows that God is not like us.

MONDAY OF THE FOURTH WEEK
OF EASTER
And the night shall be as bright as the day

'O Lord, you have searched me out and known me,' begins Psalm 139 in its description of God as the one from whom we can never escape, who holds us always before him, the one to whom all hearts are open, all desires known, and from whom no secrets are hidden. The writer wants to escape from God, however, perhaps because of an awareness of unworthiness and sin, but knows it is impossible to flee from the spirit of God. If I ascend to heaven, he says, you are there. If I go down to the abode of the dead, you are there. If I go to the farthest limits of the sea, flying on the wings of the morning, you are there also. If I think that the darkness will cover me, it will not, for the darkness is not dark to you; the night is as bright as the day, for darkness and light to you are both alike.

Here again we find the difference between human experience of the fear of night and the world as known by God. 'Lighten our darkness, we beseech thee, O Lord' is our prayer at Evensong, 'and by thy great mercy defend us from all perils and dangers of this night.' Darkness is our experience: darkness as a cloak for evil deeds, darkness as the bringer of death. We hate being plunged into darkness with all the fear of the unknown, the unseen, that it brings. The hell of the imagination is a dark world illuminated only by the inextinguishable fires that consume the damned; heaven is a place of light without shadow – Donne's one equal light. To celebrate the rising of Christ, the faithful gather in the dark to see the new light, the light of the resurrection, break forth on the world. The liturgy talks of 'undying radiance' and 'unfailing light' linking the Easter fire to God's own glory and praying that the mystical fire will light up our hearts and senses. It speaks of the night of the resurrection as that night of which Scripture says: 'And the night shall be as bright as day. And the night shall light up my joy.'

Let us look again at the Paschal Candle. It should be standing prominently in the church and should burn every day from Easter to Pentecost. On Good Friday every burning light, lamp and candle in church should have been extinguished and the new fire, the Easter fire, is the source of light for the whole year to come. The lights that burn before the Blessed Sacrament and before various altars should be lit from it. Matches should really be banished from the church and every light that is lit should take the Paschal Candle as its source. It reminds us constantly of how the risen Christ is the source of our life and our salvation and how we, who received the lighted candle at our baptism and held a burning flame when we renewed our baptismal covenant, should shine in the world with Christ's light. As the Exsultet says, the flame is divided without suffering any loss of light as it is spread among us.

It should be a wonderful pillar of beeswax, marked with the sign of the cross, carrying the Greek letters alpha and omega and the numerals of the year, and pierced by the incense grains that represent Christ's wounds. Using a plastic casing with a gas flame, or reusing last year's candle, destroys the powerful symbolism of the liturgy. When I see the candle burning alone in the darkened church, I am always amazed at how much light one candle, albeit a very large candle, produces. It pushes back the darkness. This candle will be consumed by its daily burning, until it is little more than a stump placed beside the font, but its light continues to burn in the hearts of believers.

TUESDAY OF THE FOURTH WEEK
OF EASTER
God saw that it was good

The vigil readings, known as the Prophecies, set out the story of salvation. There were originally twelve of them but as time has gone on the number that have to be read has been reduced. Contemporary liturgical books require just four, which must include part of Exodus 14. The first of the readings is the account of creation in Genesis 1 and the first verses of chapter 2. It provides the context for everything that follows. God created the world. To say that this was so, that in the beginning of all things it was God who created the heaven and the earth, is not to bring Christianity into conflict with science. Genesis is not making a scientific claim but setting out the relation between the creation, the creatures and the Creator. That this affirmation is essential to the whole Christian faith is amply demonstrated by its inclusion in the creed we say at the Eucharist, the so-called Nicene Creed. We state our belief in 'God the Father Almighty, maker of heaven and earth, of all things, visible and invisible.'

Creation begins with darkness; with earth as a void, and empty waste, a watery abyss. Over the waters there brooded the Spirit of God. And the first act of creation is God speaking. 'Let there be light,' says God, and so the light began, and the light pushed back the darkness. God found that the light was good and divided light from darkness, calling the light Day and the darkness Night. The history of humankind can be seen as the return of the darkness and its encroachment into the realm of light, hence the need for the light of Christ that turns the darkness into light and makes the night as bright as the day.

Genesis 1 goes on to describe each of the days of creation, the evening and the morning being one day. That is why the Christian day, and the Jewish day before it, goes from evening to evening, because Genesis says 'so evening came and morning' in that order. On the first day the light is created; on the second the waters are pushed back and the sky is created; on the third the waters are again pushed back and dry land appears, and this is followed by the earth producing grasses and fruit trees, each with power to propagate its own; on the fourth day God made two great lights, 'the greater one to rule the day, the lesser one to rule the night'; on the fifth the sea creatures and the birds came into being; on the sixth different kinds of living things on the land, 'cattle and creeping things and wild beasts of every sort' and finally, and on the same day, God said:

> 'Let us make humankind in our image, according to our likeness; and let them have dominion over the fish of the sea, and over the birds of the air, and over the cattle, and over all the wild animals of the earth, and over every creeping thing that creeps upon the earth.'

> So God created humankind in his image,
> in the image of God he created them;
> male and female he created them.

> God blessed them, and God said to them, 'Be fruitful and multiply, and fill the earth and subdue it; and have dominion over the fish of the sea and over the birds of the air and over every living thing that moves upon the earth' (Genesis 1.26–8).

And God saw all that he had made, and found it very good. So the sixth day passed and all was finished and the seventh day God rested with his whole task accomplished.

This, then, is the beginning of all things, each in its proper place and order. The vigil readings will not go on to tell of the fall of Adam and Eve, as we are used to from carol services, but will go on to look at what happened when human beings spread across the face of the earth. After the creation we turn at once to Noah.

WEDNESDAY OF THE FOURTH WEEK OF EASTER
The ark rode safe on the waters

Although at the end of creation God looked upon what he had made and saw that it was good, when the Almighty surveyed the scene again in the days of Noah much had changed. The world was corrupt in God's sight. Every creature had turned away and lost its true direction, the true purpose of its existence. God found 'that the earth was full of men's iniquities and that the whole frame of their thought was set continually on evil' (Genesis 6.11). God does not examine what has gone wrong, but because he sees that both human beings and the rest of the creation have departed from their true directions, he regrets having made them at all and resolves to blot them out from the earth by allowing the waters to return. There is a sense of sadness as God finds that the creation is no longer good, but as he scans the earth seeking some exception from the prevailing rule of depravity and corruption he finds Noah and Noah's sons, Shem, Ham and Japheth. Noah is without fault and God decides that he and his wife and his sons and their wives should survive and enable a new beginning to be made. With Noah God makes the first covenant. He makes it before the flood as he gives instruction for the building of the ark.

The account of the destruction of the earth is a dramatic reversal of the story of creation. The waters that are held back break through, coming up from the depths, at the same time as the flood-gates of heaven are opened. The rain pours for forty days and forty nights, rising higher and higher, and carrying the ark upwards with it. The water rises until it covers the mountains, until it is impossible for any creature to survive, and it stays at this high flood level for one hundred and fifty days. And then God thought on Noah, and his spirit again passed over the waters, as it had done in the beginning, and the water abated. The rains stopped, the springs were closed up; the flood-gates shut. It takes time, however, for the earth to dry out, and Noah tests several times before he establishes that the water is shallow and that trees and plants are again appearing. Finally, and once more at God's word, Noah and his family and all the creatures emerge from the ark, and God tells them to occupy the earth, to increase and multiply upon it. The first thing that Noah does is to offer a sweet-smelling sacrifice of thanksgiving to the Lord.

This is, in its way, a new creation out of the water that took away life from the earth but also preserved it. We cannot escape the story of Noah being a story of judgement and of destruction by God of what was judged unworthy, but this theme of judgement and destruction is one that is repeated throughout Scripture and the liturgy. The writer to the Hebrews says: 'By faith Noah, warned by God about events as yet unseen, respected the warning and built an ark to save his household; by this he condemned the world and became an heir to righteousness that is in accordance with faith' (Hebrews 11.7). It is never total condemnation and destruction, however, for the sovereign will of God brings forth a remnant and looks constantly for a new beginning. It is not a new creation *ex nihilo*, like the first creation, but one that continues by redemption what has already come into being.

The Easter liturgy links the ark to the Church; it also links the flood to baptism as the new flood that destroys the old man and the former sin-laden humanity and brings about a new creation. The collect after the reading calls the Church 'a wonderful sacrament', that is an outward and visible sign of God's hidden, spiritual work. We have passed the idea of destruction and there is no turning back. Christ, in whom all things had their beginning, is even now bringing things to perfection in him. Whatever we may think at any given time about the state of the world, God has shown that human history will end well and calls us to live confidently. 'May the whole world feel and see', says the collect, 'the downcast lifted up, worn-out things renewed and all things returning to their perfection'.

THURSDAY OF THE FOURTH WEEK
OF EASTER
Abraham! Abraham!

The story of Abraham occupies chapters 12–24 of Genesis. From out of the story the Easter liturgy takes only one section, the best-known incident in the life of the patriarch – God's request that he should offer his son Isaac in sacrifice. Abraham's sacrifice was one of the favourite subjects in early Christian art and at least since the fourth century it has appeared as a type of the sacrifice of the Cross, and hence also of the eucharistic sacrifice. Isaac is like Christ – he is the child of promise, his birth is greeted with laughter and rejoicing; he is the rightful inheritor, displacing Hagar's son, and he himself carries the wood of sacrifice. He is also unlike Christ – notably because he is born of a barren woman, not of a virgin, and his sacrifice, though staged, is not accomplished.

Inevitably Christian commentators noted this relationship and the way in which Isaac pointed to that sacrifice that was reserved for Christ. They noted that Isaac bore the wood but they focused on what God provided, the ram caught in the thicket by its horns, the ram that was then offered in sacrifice. The thicket was seen as a foreshadowing of the crown of thorns; the way the ram hung there a foreshadowing of Christ hanging on the tree. The Greek fathers saw Isaac as representing the indestructible divinity of Christ and the ram his human nature which was sacrificed. Two examples will do, first Gregory of Nyssa:

> The whole mystery of faith can be seen in the story of Isaac. The lamb is fixed to the tree, suspended by its horns:

the first-born carries upon him the wood of sacrifice. He, then, who upholds the universe by the word of his power, is the same who bears the burden of our wood, and is hung up on the wood, upholding as God, and carried as the lamb, the Holy Spirit having in figure divided the mystery between the two, the only son and the lamb who appears at his side. In the lamb is revealed the mystery of death and in the only son the life which will never be cut short by death.

Second, St John Chrysostom:

All these things were types of the cross. That is why Christ said: Abraham rejoiced that he might see my day: he saw it, and was glad. How did he see it, considering that he was born so many years before? He saw it in type and in shadow. A lamb was offered for Isaac, and a spiritual lamb was offered for the world. The reality had to be depicted beforehand in type. Consider, I beg you, to what extent everything has been told in advance. In both instances we have an only son; in both instances one who is greatly loved. The first was offered as a victim by his father, and so was the latter offered by the Father. The type carries us a long way, but how much further does the reality go.

(*Homilies*)

And what of Abraham? This incident, called Akedah, from the Hebrew stem 'to bind', brings the story of Abraham near to its conclusion. At the outset Abraham was to leave his father's house, now he is to sacrifice his son, as he had previously surrendered Ishmael. Both sons are saved by divine intervention. But central to it all is Abraham's spiritual journey that so powerfully expresses his unwavering faith in God. Abraham has questioned God's justice before; he does not question it now. The three-day journey – three days meaning a lengthy period – shows that this is an act of free will, not merely an impulsive response. The conversation between father and son is limited but there is an evident bond of trust between them and the bond remains unbroken as the truth seems to dawn on Isaac. The detailed matter-of-fact description of the preparation for the sacrifice, preparation made without conversation, and leading to the point where Abraham puts forth his hand to take the knife and slay his son, conveys something of the eternity of that terrible moment before the angelic voice is heard. We know it is to come. Abraham and Isaac did not. On Calvary's hill it does not come at all. Abraham is here vindicated by intention and by act as the God-fearing man who surrenders to the divine will, and so God reaffirms his promise.

FRIDAY OF THE FOURTH WEEK
OF EASTER
Stretch out your hand over the sea

Anciently the Easter vigil included the celebration of baptism
and the readings are a commentary on baptismal symbolism.
Some of them set out the 'types' of baptism, that is to say its
anticipation in certain Old Testament passages. So, the creation
emerges from the primeval waters and Noah is saved by the
floating ark; in the fourth Prophecy we come to the crossing
of the Red Sea. It is one of the most wonderful moments in
the account of the Exodus. The Israelites were afraid as they
found themselves caught between Pharaoh's chariots and the
sea, and Moses tells them not to fear but to stand firm and to
see 'the salvation of the Lord, which he will work for you
today'. The pillar of cloud shielded the Israelites from the
sight of the Egyptians during the night and then Moses lifted
his rod and stretched out his hand over the sea and the Lord
divided the waters creating dry land. 'And the people of Israel
went into the midst of the sea on dry ground, the waters
being a wall to them on their right hand and on their left.'
The Egyptians – 'all Pharaoh's horses, his chariots, and his
horsemen' – followed after them into the midst of the sea.
This is the point at which the Prophecy took up the story.

In the morning watch the Lord looked down from the
pillar of fire and of cloud and saw the Egyptians and he
brought about their doom. First, he clogged the chariot
wheels, so that the charioteers panicked and cried that they
should go back because the Lord was fighting against them.
At that moment God told Moses, 'Stretch out your hand over

the sea, that the water may come back upon the Egyptians, upon their chariots and their horsemen.' This Moses did and the waters returned to their place and 'the Lord routed the Egyptians in the midst of the sea'. Not so much as one of them remained.

This reading is followed by the singing of the song of triumph of Moses and the Israelites that begins 'I will sing to the Lord for he has triumphed gloriously; the horse and his rider he has thrown into the sea.' There is a version of it set as a canticle in *Common Worship*; it is edited to remove the difficult parts. It becomes a song of praise to the right hand of the Lord which 'glorious in power . . . shatters the enemy' but it finds difficulty with the drowning of Pharaoh's chariots and his host. Perhaps it is a consequence of the endless killing that marked the twentieth century that Christians have become wary of some of the divine acts of power recorded in the Old Testament. The Exodus was marked by considerable violence as Israel escaped from Egypt and entered into the Promised Land subduing and slaughtering many peoples along the way. We can read it symbolically as the subjection of evil – Egypt represents evil and the worship of false gods – but to read it literally as a version of history is very difficult. God is merciless as he presses the claims of his people. Those who worshipped other gods were to be ousted from the land, their idols and altars destroyed, and they themselves were, if necessary, to be sacrificed. Religious tolerance abhors such an unwillingness to cohabit with those who hold another religion in good faith. A fierce monotheistic iconoclast religion sees this cleansing as utterly necessary. If we are committed to the preservation of the world's cultural heritage, we must decry the destruction of 2,000-year-old statues of the Buddha in Afghanistan, but when we read our own Scriptures we may understand something more of the spirit that animates such religious fervour.

Another liturgical commentator, the German Benedictine nun Aemiliana Löhr, makes a helpful observation about these readings. By the lectern from which these Prophecies are read the Paschal Candle is burning; its light falls upon the pages of the Old Testament. Christ casts his light into the darkness of the past, and shows there the design of his love. In the context of the Easter liturgy the story of the Red Sea is a type of baptism: the old is drowned in the sea and there emerges from it a new creation.

Search for the Lord while he wills to be found

Dame Aemiliana goes on to remind us that the Fathers of the
Church held, against those who would have abandoned the
Old Testament, that the whole of these ancient scriptures, all
the events and all the figures, are prophecies looking forward
to Christ. It is not just the properly prophetic books that
perform this function, but Christ is announced through
people and things and events. And the Church sees the Old
Testament as part of the oneness of God's revelation, moving
in a straight line from Adam to Christ and reaching its fullness in him. This function of the Old Testament is most
obvious at Easter and we should give it our full attention,
remembering how Jesus, beginning with Moses and all the
prophets, interpreted to the disciples on the road to Emmaus
'in all the Scriptures the things concerning himself.' The four
lessons from Genesis and Exodus are followed by four from
the prophetic books Isaiah, Baruch, Ezekiel and Isaiah again,
in which the Church is seen as the inheritor of the promises
to Israel.

The first of these comes from Isaiah 54.17b—55.11. It is
a statement of Israel's inheritance and an invitation to participate freely in good things, in water, milk and wine, and
abundant food. You may imagine how this sounded to a
congregation who had spent forty days in real fasting – not
just abstinence from alcohol and chocolate – and had experienced the liturgy of the Passion, and it must have been even
more significant for those who were preparing for baptism.

The divine invitation rings out, calling all who will hear to hear as God calls them into his love. The summons is urgent, for only if we hear the Word of God and respond to it can our souls have life. In this call to his people, God renews the covenant and makes David, and David's son, the witness to the peoples and the leader and commander of all the peoples God calls.

The twentieth century developed a profound sense of the absence of God. The Holy One seemed harder to find than in previous ages, and at the moments when one expected to find him, he wasn't there. The more it was stressed that God, like a loving father, cared for his children, the more the sense of being orphaned increased until it ended in passionate rejection of God and denial of the possibility of belief in God. If there was a God and he was omnipotent, how could he allow the slaughter in the trenches, in the camps and in the gulags? And, as I so often heard, how could he allow the innocent, especially children, to die painfully? Those of a different and perhaps deeper spirituality saw that the optimism of nineteenth-century missionary Christianity was very shallow and that the heart of the faith was to be found in the Lord's Passion. God was in the midst of the orgy of killing that marked the century, clearly present as the crucified Redeemer, who went not up to joy before first he suffered pain and entered not into glory before he was crucified.

'Seek the Lord while he may be found, call upon him while he is near.' This is what the prophet declares and in doing so reminds us of what we already knew – there are times when God seems very distant and inaccessible, when we are profoundly aware of the distance between the creature and the Creator, between the mortal and the immortal. Isaiah reinforces this. God is not made in our image. His thoughts are not our thoughts; his ways are not our ways. We have neither the right nor the ability to judge God. The distance between us is too great. But God condescends to us. We use 'condescending' to mean 'patronizing'. It really means stooping down to a lower level, and in theological terms it refers to the entirely free and gracious way that God comes down to us. 'How wonderful the condescension of thy mercy towards us,' says the Exsultet, 'how far beyond all reckoning thy loving-kindness! To ransom thy slave, thou gavest up thy Son!' The liturgy celebrates this condescension on two occasions, on two holy nights when heaven and earth touch and the light of God illumines human darkness: Christmas night and Easter night. On these nights above all other nights God wills to be found and calls on us to return to him that he may have mercy on us.

SUNDAY OF THE FIFTH WEEK
OF EASTER
Who can tell where wisdom dwells?

The sixth Prophecy comes from Baruch, a book in the Apocrypha which, together with Lamentations, forms a sort of appendix to the book of Jeremiah. The history of the book is rather complex. It claims to have been written by Baruch, Jeremiah's disciple at the time of the Jewish exile in Babylon, but scholars think that it is much later than that, from the period after the Maccabean revolt, and in the Jewish liturgy it provides a cycle of Sabbath readings that commemorate national disasters. These began to be used after the fall of Jerusalem in AD 70.

Baruch 3.9–37 addresses the Israelites as those living in the land of their enemies, growing old in a foreign country, a way of living hardly better than being dead. The reason, Baruch tells them, is that they have forsaken the fountain of wisdom and have not walked in the way of God. 'Learn where there is wisdom,' he says, 'where there is strength, where there is understanding, that you may at the same time discern where there is length of days, and life, where there is light for the eyes and peace.' Many seek after wisdom but do not find her because she is not to be found by human effort. Wisdom comes from God and from God alone. Baruch shows that God bestows this gift wherever he wills:

> This is our God; no other can be compared to him!
> He found the whole way to knowledge,
> and gave her to Jacob his servant

and to Israel whom he loved.
Afterwards she appeared upon earth and lived
    among men.

We must recall how the Paschal Light illumines the pages of
Scripture and how the liturgical celebration of the mysteries
of salvation forms a seamless whole. Incarnation and redemption are two sides of the same coin. Here again on Easter
night we recall Christmas night. Wisdom and Word are one.
The Word became flesh and dwelt among us. Wisdom was
revealed on earth and held converse with mortals. As the old
introit of the Mass of the Sunday after Christmas said: 'While
all around lay deep in sleep, and night had no more than
passed the middle point of her journey, then, Lord, thy
almighty Word came down from thy royal throne.' The Easter
liturgy reinforces the way in which God went beyond the
dramatic manifestation of divine power to enter into converse
with human beings. The incarnation initiates a new and
definitive phase in the conversation between the creation and
the Creator; the full meaning of this discourse unfolds in the
Passion and Resurrection of the Incarnate Word.

MONDAY OF THE FIFTH WEEK
OF EASTER
Prophesy to the bones, Son of man

Long sequences of readings can be very tiring, especially when they concern abstract or complex ideas. By the seventh Prophecy tiredness is setting in and sleep drifts over the faithful. This is the time for a story, and no story is more likely to wake the sleeper than that of Ezekiel in the valley of the dry bones, contained in Ezekiel 37. The image is wonderful. The prophet is transported and set down in a valley full of bones and the bones were very dry. God asks: 'Can these bones live?' and the prophet wisely answers 'O Lord God, thou knowest.' He is then told, in words that might well cause us to break into song, to prophesy to the bones and to say to them 'O dry bones, hear the word of the Lord.' The verses that follow provided an account that inspired artists who had to depict the general resurrection on the last day. There was a noise and a rattling and the bones started to come together, bone linking to bone, and then, as the prophet watched, there came sinews and flesh and skin, but no breath. The prophet was again called upon to prophesy and to summon the four winds to breathe into the slain, and at this command the enfleshed bones lived and stood upon their feet. This was all a sign of what God would do for the whole house of Israel:

> Thus says the Lord God:
> Behold, I will open your graves,
> and raise you from your graves, O my people;
> and I will bring you home into the land of Israel.

And you shall know that I am the Lord,
when I open your graves,
and raise you from your graves, O my people.
(Ezekiel 37.12–13)

Read in the old Paschal Vigil this was a prophecy not to the
old Israel but to the new Israel, the Church. Humankind is
alienated from the source of life by sin; it is thus destined
to death. The valley of dry bones is a biblical image that
relates to our experience of the mass graves of those slaugh-
tered in the twentieth century in war, in the persecution of
the Jews, in the various attempts at so-called ethnic cleansing.
Humankind seems wedded to death. The Church is a people
who, through Christ, have caught hold of everlasting life.
Baptized into Christ's death, the faithful share in his resurrection. The Word and Wisdom of God, the incarnate Christ,
tells his disciples in a farewell discourse in John (14.18–19)
that he will not leave them desolate – 'because I live, you will
live also'. And the risen Christ breathes on the disciples and
fills them with the Holy Spirit, the breath of life. This part
of the vigil was especially addressed to those about to be
baptized and who were to receive that same Holy Spirit.

TUESDAY OF THE FIFTH WEEK
OF EASTER
Sion's remnant

The last of this group of four prophecies takes us back to Isaiah (4.1–6). The first verse is really a conclusion to chapter 3, a prophecy of judgement against Judah and Jerusalem. So many of the men of Israel have perished that there are seven women to every man and as the reading opens they take hold of a man and ask nothing of him except that they shall be called by his name and lose the reproach that has fallen upon them. But the prophet then tells what the Lord will do for those who remain and it is a beautiful vision of filth washed away and bloodstains removed, with Zion restored to holiness. Over all things there will be, as there was when Israel came out of Egypt, a cloud by day and smoke and a shining flame of fire by night. As the Church gathers around the Paschal Candle this is seen as a prophecy that reinforces her sense of being chosen, of being the true remnant of Sion.

As the story of Israel crossing the Red Sea led into Moses' song of triumph, so this eighth reading led into Isaiah's song of the vineyard. The importance of the vineyard became apparent before Jesus' Passion. After his argument with the Pharisees about his authority, he began to tell the people a parable (Luke 20.9): 'A man planted a vineyard and let it out to tenants . . .' As Jesus tells this beautifully crafted little story, the religious leaders are listening. They are men of knowledge. Their vision may not be great; their own self-importance has got in the way of true knowledge of God. Nevertheless, they are thoroughly versed in the Scriptures. They hear every nuance, grasp every reference, every echo of another text, wherever it is to be found in the Law and the Prophets. 'A man planted a vineyard,' says Jesus. A vineyard, think the teachers of Israel. There are rules in the Law about vineyards and the gleaning of grapes. There is the story of Naboth and his vineyard, of Ahab's covetousness and Jezebel's plot, of Elijah's rebuke and of the death of Ahab and Jezebel. There is the good wife who plants a vineyard with her own hands and the vineyard of Solomon in the Song of Songs. But there is another vineyard that provides the key to Jesus' parable and I dare say they knew at once. It is Isaiah's song found in the Paschal Vigil.

'Let me sing for my beloved a love song concerning his vineyard. My beloved had a vineyard on a very fertile hill.' He digged it and cleared it of stones and planted it with choice vines, but it yielded wild grapes. And now, O inhabitants of Jerusalem, judge I pray you between me and my vineyard. The result of that judgement was destruction: the hedge removed and the wall broken down. I will make it a waste, says the prophet; it shall not be pruned or hoed and briars and thorns shall grow up. For the vineyard of the Lord of hosts is the house of Israel, and he, the Lord of hosts, looked for justice, but behold, bloodshed; for righteousness, but behold, a cry! The leaders of the Jews knew Jesus told the parable against them for they knew Isaiah's song.

For the Church it means something quite different; it is not a reproach but a blessing, for Christ said to his disciples, 'I am the vine; you are the branches.' There is no fear as the Church hears the chant for she knows that she is the vineyard of the Lord of hosts and will bring forth abundant fruit. The concluding collect sums up her thoughts and prayers. God is the sower of good seed and the cultivator of choice vine-shoots. The Church asks that among those peoples who are the Lord's vineyards the rubbish of thorns and briars may be cleared away so that they may bring forth worthy and abundant fruit.

WEDNESDAY OF THE FIFTH WEEK
OF EASTER
It is the night of the Lord's Passover

The ninth Prophecy may come as a surprise. A note of great seriousness returns to the liturgy with the reading from Exodus 12.1–11. This is the account of the institution of the Passover. On the tenth day of the first month of the year all the congregation of Israel are to take a lamb from the flock, a sheep or a goat, without blemish, male, one year old. On the fourteenth day in the evening all the lambs were to be slain and the blood was to be put on the doorposts and the lintels of the houses. The flesh of the lamb was to be eaten that night, roasted and eaten with unleavened bread and bitter herbs. And those who ate it were to have their loins girded, their sandals on their feet and staff in hand. They were to eat in haste – 'It is the night of the Pasch, the Lord's passing by.' In the old Good Friday liturgy this reading preceded the reading of the Passion. Its meaning was inescapable. It was then to be read again on Holy Saturday night and we can therefore see how context in the liturgy affects the meaning of a passage. On Friday the focus is on the lamb that is slain; on Saturday we see how the blood of the lamb protects believers. Christ, the true Paschal Lamb, marks the house of the faithful, the Church, with his blood, and so keeps them safe from God's wrath. The reading looks forward to the singing of the Easter sequence *Victimae paschali laudes*:

> Christians to the paschal Victim
> offer sacrifice and praise.

> The sheep are ransomed by the Lamb;
> and Christ, the undefiled, hath sinners
> to his Father reconciled.

The collect that followed this prophecy picks up a theme already set out in the first collect, in its reference to God having wondrously fashioned us and yet more wondrously redeemed us:

> Almighty, everlasting God,
> who art wonderful in the plan of all thy works,
> let those whom thou hast redeemed understand
> that the creation of the world in the beginning
> was not a more excellent thing than the sacrifice of Christ,
> our Easter victim, at the climax of the ages.

THURSDAY OF THE FIFTH WEEK
OF EASTER
Nineveh, that great city

Sometimes the liturgy expects more of us than we are able to give, for our knowledge of Scripture is today so limited, and the parts we know by heart even more so, that we do not pick up on the cross-references, the echoes of other texts. Jesus several times mentions Jonah and the great fish. The tenth Prophecy from the old Easter vigil carries on with that story from after the point when Jonah was vomited up on dry land (Jonah 3.1–10). It tells of how Jonah went to Nineveh, 'an exceeding great city, three days' journey in breadth', and began to preach that in forty days the city would be over-thrown. The people of Nineveh, rather unexpectedly, believed what the prophet said, repented in sackcloth and ashes and were saved from God's fierce anger (something that did not please Jonah!). As Christ was seen as the true Passover lamb, he is here seen as the new Jonah who comes back from the belly of the world below and, as the risen one, calls upon the heathen to return and live for God. As the French Oratorian Father Louis Bouyer pointed out, this reading is directed both to the wider non-believing world, as God extends the Gospel to all humanity, and then towards those who will shortly be baptized. Those awaiting baptism are reminded that God expects active repentance as the sign of faith but that he provides the grace that is necessary for our words to become actions. 'Grant us,' asks the collect, 'both the will and the power to do what thou commandest.'

FRIDAY OF THE FIFTH WEEK
OF EASTER
The last testament of Moses

❧

There are only two Prophecies to go and the long vigil will
reach its climax with the blessing of the font and the celebration of Holy Baptism. The penultimate reading is the
account of Moses' last testimony in Deuteronomy 31.22–30.
Preparing for his death, he set down the Law and had the
book laid up by the side of the ark. Moses had never forgot-
ten that the Israelites were rebellious and stiff-necked; that
is to say, obstinate, stubborn, inflexible and haughty. He knew
only too well that even with Moses in their midst they
rebelled against God. He was sure it would be even worse
once he was gone from them. In Deuteronomy Moses calls
the elders and the officers of the tribes and speaks to them
the words of a song. It is a long song and the Easter liturgy
used but a fragment of it as a chant. In its full form it sets
down all the wonders God has done and records the rebellion of his people. The chant calls upon the chosen people to
praise the greatness of God: 'God's works are perfect, and all
his ways are just. God is faithful, in him there is no iniquity:
the Lord is just and holy.'

   Why is it placed here? Well, it comes as those to be baptized
come very close to the moment of Christian commitment.
To deny Christ after baptism is to become an apostate, one
who denies the faith one has embraced. The early Church
took a very dim view of post-baptismal sin and this Prophecy
with its chant formed both an encouragement to fidelity and
a sort of warning against rebellion. It was thought that there

was no way of being reconciled after baptism, for one could not be baptized again, but the Church came to take seriously the promise that the risen Christ made to his Church concerning the forgiveness of sins. Hence the Christian has available the sacrament of reconciliation, also known as penance or as confession and absolution. The prayer that concludes this section contained an interesting petition: Give joy, diminish fear. Christianity is not a religion of fear. We are not supposed to live in fear of hell and damnation. The governing principle of our lives should be love, love of God and love of neighbour, awareness of God's love for us and response to it. It is right, of course, to remind those who as responsible adults make the commitment involved in baptism that it is not something to be done half-heartedly, but the Church asks that the faithful should have joy in believing and should not be oppressed by fear. Perfect love casts out fear. The Easter liturgy as it unfolds God's love for us facilitates our response to that love.

SATURDAY OF THE FIFTH WEEK
OF EASTER
The fiery furnace

The last Prophecy returns us dramatically to storytelling in its finest oriental form. It is the tale of the fiery furnace in Daniel 3.1–24. Shadrach, Meshach and Abednego are three young Jewish men who refuse to obey King Nebuchadnezzar's order concerning the great statue of himself that he has made. They refuse to bow down to it and worship it even when he threatens them with being cast into a raging fiery furnace. 'You are in my power,' says the king, 'What God can deliver you?' The three young men answer that the king will see for himself that their God will rescue them from the furnace. The king fell into a fury and ordered the furnace to be made even hotter than usual, so hot that the guards who threw them in were themselves incinerated. Shadrach, Meshach and Abednego were cast in bound and clothed in 'breeches and turban, shoes and coat', but they were soon seen walking about in the heart of the flames, singing to God their praises, blessing the Lord. As Jonah comes forth from the belly of the fish, so the three young men come out of the fiery furnace, and that emergence makes it another 'type' of the resurrection.

Not only does this reading celebrate the power of God but it offers a clear message to those who have been baptized and those who are preparing for baptism. A Christian is expected to witness to the good news of Jesus Christ, to the definitive revelation of the true God in his Word and incarnate Wisdom. Anyone who witnesses must be prepared to accept suffering and even death. If we have not learned that, then we have given too little attention to the events of Holy Week. But the risen Christ watches over his Church and those who witness with their lives have a special place in the presence of God.

With this reading the old vigil ended. It was a lengthy exploration of the Creator's plan of love, showing how redemption is a part and continuation of the creation, a process by which the creation is healed and restored. Our current lectionary cycles enable us to become familiar with a wide range of biblical readings but there are certain curious omissions, stories familiar of old are now hardly heard or else heard at such a time that their voice is muted.

SUNDAY OF THE SIXTH WEEK
OF EASTER
The brimming font

Those who were waiting to be baptized would, at this point in the Paschal Liturgy, have come to the font. The choir would have sung *Sicut cervus* – 'O God, my soul longs for thee, as a deer for running water'. The theme of this psalm is familiar to us from the hymn 'As pants the hart for cooling streams when heated in the chase, so longs my heart for thee, O God.' It is expected that the candidates have long desired to make their profession of faith and to be baptized in Christ's dying and rising, that they have longed for this union with Christ. The time has now come.

The old rite, reformed after the Second Vatican Council, was a long and complex one. It recalled the various facets of water, starting with the waters over which the Spirit brooded in the beginning and the sanctifying waters of the flood that washed away the crimes of a guilty world. The priest asked for the inpouring of divine power that would make the water of the font fruitful and make the font a womb for rebirth. It is called the fount of life, the water of new birth, a purifying stream, and in a further section the priest recalls the four streams that flowed out of paradise, the bitter water in the desert that was made sweet, and the rock from which water gushed, and then the water that Jesus turned to wine at Cana, the water upon which he walked and that with which he was baptized, leading to that which, with blood, flowed from his side, and ending with his command to the disciples to baptize those to whom they brought the gospel. The blessing included the dipping of the Paschal Candle into the font and the adding to the water of some of the holy oils consecrated on Maundy Thursday. Finally, after their long preparation and this lengthy vigil, those who professed the faith were given their final interrogations and plunged into the water of baptism, emerging to be anointed with oil, robed in white and given a candle to hold.

Here, then, the second great mystery of the vigil is unfolded. The first was the mystery of light, the light of life which shatters the darkness of death. The second is the mystery of life-giving water, the restoration of the rivers that flowed from Eden and brought life to the lands around. Christ the Light is also the source of living water, and the brimming font powerfully expresses this.

MONDAY OF THE SIXTH WEEK
OF EASTER
A spouse in blood

In the Letter to the Ephesians, chapter 5, St Paul likens the relationship of husband and wife to that of Christ and the Church. The thrust of his argument is that wives should be subject to their husbands and, less controversially, that husbands should love their wives. It is not merely by way of illustration that he uses the language of body and bride about the Church, for he is clear that Christ loves his Church as a bridegroom loves his bride.

The marriage theme with its stress on unity and love is already prepared in the Old Testament. The divine Word, the creating power that goes forth from God, loves the humanity it has brought into being. Wisdom celebrates a marriage with humankind. In the epistle the image is reversed: Wisdom is the bride, the fairest of women, to be sought and courted, a pearl of great price. Christians have always found in the Song of Songs, the canticle of the lover and the beloved, an expression and celebration of the love between Christ and his Church.

The divine lover is Christ and the beloved of his choice is the Church. John the Baptist calls himself the bridegroom's friend, the best man. He stands at the bridegroom's side, he hears his voice and rejoices to hear it. Like many a best man, he undertakes preparations for the wedding, and does so with joy. When the day of the wedding comes, it is the bride and groom who stand in the light, and not the best man. Jesus uses very similar language. So long as the bridegroom is with them, the disciples have no need to fast and mourn, but rejoice at the glad tidings. Jesus warns that one day the bridegroom will be taken away, and then will come the time for fasting and sorrow. Then the bride is left alone with her burning longing for the beloved, and her loneliness may last for a long time, for no one can tell when the bridegroom returns. The great banquet, the wedding feast, the marriage feast of the Lamb, of which the Scriptures so often speak, belonged to the end of time, when all things are fulfilled.

This image of the Church as the bride of Christ is not simply a way of speaking, a metaphorical or analogical way of expressing a deep, complex and little-understood relationship. As we hear it set forth we are intended to find in it the symbols and shadows and echoes that express and spring from our own experience of love and of marriage. But there is more. The Church is a spouse of blood, or rather a spouse whose marriage, whose mystical union is made in blood. The cross is the place of consummation of this marriage and its fulfilment, the marriage of the Lamb, is foretold by John in the Revelation. The lover of the Church is also her redeemer. His wooing cost him his life. She was won, made his, purchased at a most costly price. She becomes what she is, the bride destined for the bridegroom, as a result of the shedding of his blood. This is her baptism, the source of her life, her love, her fruitfulness.

TUESDAY OF THE SIXTH WEEK
OF EASTER
I was redeemed by your blood

❦

The Church is a spouse in blood. In his sermons on the Song of Songs, the Cistercian monk John of Ford gives the Church these words:

> I was redeemed by your blood, washed in your blood, given your blood to drink, and by it made mystically drunk. Through it I hold within my heart the surest pledge of eternal restoration. The blood of my spouse is both the price of my redemption and the laver of my purification; it is the cup that sustains my exile and at the same time a strong incentive to my love being such a clear proof of his love.

His blood, then, is the assurance of his love, that intense love that is always at work in the Church transforming, purifying and renewing, for Christ loves the Church as much as he loves his own body which bears the marks of his Passion. But where do we find that intensity of love when the Church, the body of Christ, faces her divine lover? John of Ford again provides the bride's words: 'I whisper into my spouse's ear and his blood adorns my cheek.' A whisper, a kiss, an embrace – the language of a closeness to Christ that should mark every aspect of the Church's life as the blood of the bridegroom adorns the cheek of the bride.

The blood of Christ was shed for his Church. It is the blood which stains and adorns the Church. As Christ ascends

into heaven, he leaves his mark upon his Church. It refuses
to allow us to turn the Church into a club, a gathering of
like-minded people, a charitable organization or an agent
for social change or personal growth. The Church is the bride
of Christ, a spouse in blood whose union is renewed each
time we drink the cup of salvation. We are bound up with
Christ – Christ crucified – and that is a reality that touches
all that we do and all that we are, and compels us to look
forward to the fulfilment of that union, the marriage feast of
the Lamb.

WEDNESDAY OF THE SIXTH WEEK
OF EASTER
With the Father

Where was Jesus during the forty days after Easter, during those days in which he appeared to the disciples? Was he hiding somewhere? Was he alone in some place, moving between the area around Jerusalem and the safer hiding-places of Galilee? Did he come from this hiding-place to visit the disciples? 'No' is the answer. During the forty days he was 'with the Father'. It was 'from there' – in so far as 'there' was a place – that he made himself present, visible and tangible.

So did Jesus ascend to heaven immediately after his resurrection? Think for a moment of the encounter with Mary Magdalene on the morning of Easter. Jesus tells her – in the oft-repeated words *Noli me tangere* – not to cling to him. Things are no longer as they were before. The ordinary intimacy of the earth is over. Jesus' place is now with the Father. He speaks to her of his ascension: 'I have not yet ascended . . . Go to my brethren and say to them, I am ascending to my Father and your Father, to my God and your God.' These words are open to a variety of interpretations, but the central message seems clear. This true resurrection, this resurrection which is of a different order to the resurrections or resuscitations of Jairus's daughter, the widow's only son, and the beloved Lazarus, this resurrection implies, perhaps even requires, being with the Father. But the New Testament does contain different ways of expressing this, and there is a significant difference between John and Luke. This should not surprise us. As I have said before, human language fails, because it is pushed to its limits and strains, when dealing with the divine nature; and the ascension is a feature of the internal relationship between the Father and the Son.

John ties the ascension and glorification of Christ to the resurrection. Luke keeps it separate, giving rise to the feast of the Ascension, forty days after Easter. Luke gives a dramatic visual expression to ascension. After farewell words and a farewell blessing Jesus did not simply disappear, as he did at the supper at Emmaus, he departs visibly into the clouds. The resurrection appearances stress 'It is I; I am with you', but here, at the end, we see Jesus going to the Father.

And here language deserts us. The Gospel does not suggest that, having passed into a cloud, Jesus carried on through the atmosphere until he came to the Father. Christ's glorified humanity does not move as we do and does not accelerate heavenwards like a Saturn V. Neither the Father nor heaven are 'above' in a spatial sense, and the Father is not bound by place. What Scripture affirms is that Jesus in his humanity is with the Father. He is fully human; he has a body, though that body is now a glorified body, what Aquinas called a 'subtle body' no longer dragged down by its material element. We do not know the nature of his heavenly existence. It is the beginning of a new creation in which we come to participate. We do not yet live fully in that new creation – ours is the mean time and not the end time – and so the states and qualities which it involves are unknown to us. We must be satisfied with the metaphorical and figurative language that says that Jesus is 'sitting at the right hand of the Father', even though the Father has no 'right hand' as we understand it. But it is not really so hard for us to grasp the glory and the love indicated by this expression.

THE ASCENSION
God has gone up with a shout!

I love the note of triumph that finally pervades the Church in Ascensiontide. Perhaps it is so contagious because it is combined with longer and longer evenings and – we always hope – with sunshine. I love the proclamation that Christ, raised from the dead, sits at the right hand of the Father in the heavenly places, far above all rule and authority and power and dominion. I see a triumph – that great procession of veteran legionaries and captive barbarians that Rome conferred upon its heroes. Like some early Lord Mayor's Show, it culminated in the appearance of the conqueror in a gilded chariot drawn by white horses, his head adorned with the laurel wreath. In the Museum of Fine Arts in Boston, Massachusetts, I saw such wreaths a year or two ago, the product of excavations in Dacia – each of them was a great treasure, a circlet of marvellous golden leaves, the victor's crown. And the triumph is a time not for critical evaluation and serious comment but a time for trumpets to blast, choirs to sing and jubilant crowds to shout 'Alleluia!' God has gone up with a shout and the Lord with the blast of the ram's horn.

At that point I want to stop and let celebrations continue. I do not want the triumph to turn into a discussion of how the victory was achieved and whether the achievement will be lasting. For that is what we have a tendency to do – to take the victory and to analyse it, to break it down, and perhaps to denigrate and destroy it as the media has done with so many reputations, so many heroes. Who could not write a book on the failings of Christianity, listing forced baptisms, the persecution of heretics, the burning of heresiarchs, the murder of Jews, the tragedy of the crusades, the senseless violence of religious wars, opposition to scientific advance and oppression of individuals, the abuse of women, the violation of human rights? But what of the book of the triumphs of Christianity – the assurance of grace and forgiveness, the release of countless peoples from the tyranny of magic and superstition, the preservation of learning, the glories of church architecture, sculpture, art and music, the works of literature, the care of the sick, the truce of God, the witness of the churches against oppression, the holiness of the saints, and the innumerable instances of Christian heroism and courage? We cannot tell how many daily acts of kindness stem from Christian faith.

The triumph of our God, the triumph of Christ over the destructive forces of death, has ensured that, in the long run, no matter how long the run may be, our human history, that has so often looked as if it will end badly, will end well. It may seem hard to believe sometimes but that is what the Ascension affirms, the victory of our God, and if we believed it more and, aided by the eye of faith, saw great evidence of it in our world, and claimed our own part in that victory, then, surely, its effects – which will not be perfected until the end of time, when Christ comes again to judge the living and the dead – would be yet more visible and we would not hesitate to join in the cry of triumph, the festal shout of 'Alleluia!'

FRIDAY OF THE SIXTH WEEK
OF EASTER
Go, therefore, and make disciples of all nations

Jesus gave his disciples four commandments concerning ways in which the benefits of his triumph should be available to all. Two of them are found in the great commission given to them immediately before his ascension into heaven: 'Go and make disciples of all nations, baptizing them in the name of the Father and of the Son and of the Holy Spirit.' To be faithful to Christ, the Church must always have a missionary dimension, must always proclaim the good news of salvation and give an account of Christian hope, using every available method to make disciples. It must also administer the sacraments, the holy mysteries which are the pledges of Christ's love toward us, and first among them Holy Baptism. The third command of Jesus concerns the Holy Eucharist; he says to his disciples, as he takes the bread and takes the cup, 'Do this in memory of me.' And the fourth commandment, already discussed, is known as the new commandment: 'Love one another as I have loved you.' In saying this Jesus sets a new standard for love. This is not 'love your neighbour as yourself', but take me and my love as your example, as the norm for your love of others.

Baptism places the candidate into the Easter mystery which this book celebrates. It does so by the use of four signs performed as part of the sacrament, though only one is absolutely essential: the signing with the cross, the washing in water (the essential sign), the anointing with oil and the giving of the light. Each of them, as is the nature of signs, is multivalent, holding many levels of meaning. Every ritual sign belongs within a symbolic matrix from which it takes its meaning. Every use of the cross summons up images of Christ crucified as well as those of the cross as the sign of victory, heading the procession of the people of God, but may also remind us of the countless crosses that hang around necks, some as mere ornaments, some as deliberate signs of faith. The baptismal washing recalls the baptism of Jesus by John, of the Ethiopian eunuch by Philip, of the Roman centurion Cornelius by Peter; it also recalls the water of creation, Noah's flood, the waters of the Red Sea and the water of life streaming from the Temple. But we cannot help seeing as well more mundane, quotidian washings of people and things, and being reminded of basic daily necessity, of habitual cleanliness. The anointing also summons up biblical images of the oil pouring from Aaron's head onto his beard and clothing, of Samuel anointing Saul and David as kings over Israel, of Jesus anointed with the Holy Spirit, alongside the use of oils and ointments for healing, health and beauty, and the way in which bread dipped in golden olive oil evokes memories of sunshine and of Mediterranean blue skies. And the candle recalls the symbolism of light, the conquest of darkness, the power of the Paschal Candle in the Easter liturgy, and the teaching that the candle is Christ – the wax his body, born of the Virgin Mary, the wick his most pure soul hidden within, and the light and fire signs of his divinity and so of his gift of divinity to those he claims as his own in baptism.

In the new baptism rite it is now my joy to sign the candidate with the cross and say: 'Christ claims you for his own.' Of his followers Jesus says, addressing his Father, 'All mine are yours, and yours are mine, and I have been glorified in them.' Claimed by Christ, we are made children of God and co-heirs with him, and Christ is glorified in us as we live the life of those who are baptized into his death and so participate in his resurrection.

SATURDAY OF THE SIXTH WEEK OF EASTER
Why do you stand looking into heaven?

The Christ-centred part of the liturgical calendar is the largest part. It takes us in a number of stages from the voice of the Advent prophets through Christmas, Epiphany, Candlemas, the Lenten fast and Passiontide to the crucifixion, the resurrection and the ascension of the Lord. It takes, at its longest, from the end of November to the beginning of June. At its shortest it is concluded in the first week of May. It all depends upon the date of Easter. Five or six months of the year are given over to the rehearsal of the saving work of Christ. And the remainder, punctuated by saints' days and diverse celebrations, is mostly devoted to our growth in faith and our understanding of Christ's teaching.

The ascension removes the physical presence of Christ from the material world. Christ is risen; he ascends in his resurrection-body into the heavens, and there he is glorified. He sits, as the Apostles' Creed says, at the right hand of the Father. This affirmation, says St Thomas Aquinas in his commentary on the Creed, is not to be taken literally. It is a metaphor of honour and of power. Traditionally the Church turns its attention away from the ascended Christ at this point. It hears the angelic warning – 'Ye men of Galilee, why stand ye gazing up into heaven?' It turns its attention to the mission and ministry which it has received from Christ himself. Nevertheless it begins with a moment of self-doubt. 'We beseech thee,' prays the Church anxiously, 'do not leave us comfortless, but send to us thine Holy Ghost to comfort us.'

This sense of loss was increased when the great Paschal Candle was extinguished at the end of the Gospel of the ascension or at 'he ascended' in the Creed and the faithful watched the disappearing wisp of smoke and were left without the constancy that light provided. And so the Church looked to the next event, the gift of the Holy Spirit at Pentecost.

Christ enthroned was the subject of the mosaics adorning the semi-dome of the apse in ancient churches, so that above the altar of sacrifice there might be a glimpse of heavenly glory. Medieval spirituality focused increasingly on the Passion, and some have argued that the Black Death in the 1340s induced an unhealthy concentration on death and judgement and inculcated a fear that darkened the hopefulness of the Christian faith. Attempts to restore the image of the glorified one – I think of Sutherland's great tapestry at Coventry Cathedral and Epstein's *Christus Majestas* at Llandaff Cathedral – have not been entirely successful. Nevertheless we do need to look upwards, to search the heavens with eyes of faith, to contemplate the glorified Christ as we have the crucified Christ.

SUNDAY OF THE SEVENTH WEEK
OF EASTER
Concerning Judas Iscariot

In the days immediately after the ascension, Peter addressed the company (Acts 1.15–19). We are told that about 120 people were there. Peter admits that Judas was numbered among the disciples of Jesus and had his share in their ministry, and that he was the guide to those who came to arrest Jesus. Judas's fate, says Peter, was spoken beforehand by the Holy Spirit to David – the king being here considered as a prophet – and so it had to be fulfilled. The vindictive words of Psalm 109 are cited, along with Psalm 69. The little account of what happened to Judas seems to be an insertion into the text. Judas, we are told, bought a field with the money he received from the chief priests, and he fell headlong, or else swelled up, and burst open in the middle, and his bowels gushed out. This became widely known and the field was called Akeldama, the 'Field of Blood'. Matthew's account was different. Overcome with remorse, Judas took the 30 pieces of silver back to the chief priests, confessing, 'I have sinned in betraying innocent blood.' The chief priests were unconcerned, and Judas threw down the silver in the Temple and went and hanged himself. The chief priests, unable to take the money back into the treasury, because it was blood money, bought 'the potter's field' to bury strangers in, and this, says Matthew, is why it is called the Field of Blood 'to this day'. Matthew deliberately links these events to the prophecy of Jeremiah.

The Gospel versions of the betrayal vary. John says that Satan entered Judas after he received the morsel from Jesus, and does not seem to blame the man himself. There is no kiss in the garden in John's account and Judas seems uncertain about why he is betraying him. In the Garden of Gethsemane, according to Matthew's account, when Judas came with an armed force, and greeted Jesus and kissed him, Jesus called him 'friend', but Luke says that Jesus called him by name, saying 'Judas, would you betray the Son of Man with a kiss?' No one seems very concerned about Judas, the son of Simon Iscariot, and he is never mentioned again after the first chapter of Acts, but in a way he haunts the Church. He was numbered among the disciples, he shared in their ministry; he had his feet washed by the Lord; he received the broken bread and drank from the cup; and yet he was able to betray him.

It is hard to know what motivated Judas or what he thought he would achieve, whether it was a momentary madness or a deliberate act of malice, whether Judas was the weak link used by the forces opposed to Jesus, spiritual and human, to bring about his arrest. The liturgy does not make a villain of him: that would be too easy. It is much worse that he is a friend, as the Psalmist says: 'Even my bosom friend in whom I trusted, who ate of my bread, has lifted his heel against me' (Psalm 41.9). And again: 'It is not an enemy who taunts me – then I could bear it; it is not an adversary who deals insolently with me – then I could hide from him. But it is you, my equal, my companion, my familiar friend.'

The German biblical scholar Keim says this:

The fact of the treason of Judas is so unexpected, so incredible, so terrible; it jeopardises so painfully our faith not only in human fidelity but also in the dignity and greatness of Jesus, in his knowledge, his judgement, his keen-ness of vision, and above all the weight of his influence and of the love of his which could melt even ice, and it is such a mark for the scoffing of enemies that we should have to greet it as the removal of a hundred pound weight from the heart of Christendom, if the treason of Judas could be proved to have had no existence.

('On Judas')

MONDAY OF THE SEVENTH WEEK OF EASTER
Who in the same night in which he was betrayed

'To press or touch with the lips, in token of affection, greeting, or reverence.' That is how the *Shorter Oxford Dictionary* defines the verb 'to kiss'. There is no definition of a kiss that does not involve affection. The Greek word *philos* means beloved, dear, a friend, and we find it in all those words that involve affection, like philosophy, love of *sophia*, wisdom, and the verb *phileo*, reasonably enough, means to display that affection, to do some act of kindness or affection. The Latin *osculum* has less about affection, focusing, quite literally, on the mouth – a kiss always involves the mouth, and our own word, with all its relatives in Old English and Dutch and Old High German, holds together the meanings in the Greek and the Latin – a token of affection that involves pressing or touching with the lips.

I am concerned here with one particular kiss. Scripture says: 'And the one named Judas drew near to Jesus to kiss him.' That is Luke; Mark and Matthew make it even stronger, saying he kissed affectionately, fervently or, just possibly, with much show.

There is not a great deal of kissing in Scripture, and all of it is affectionate, all except this one incident. Much of it is in Genesis in the mutual embraces of Jacob and Rachel, of Joseph and his brothers, and when Joseph weeps over his dead father and kisses him. Kissing also appears as a sign of reconciliation – David kisses Absalom, and the father kisses the prodigal son. And in the Song of Songs we pass into the frankly erotic and find kisses sweet as wine.

Only two people are actually described as kissing Jesus – though if he was as beautiful as he appears in paintings of the Madonna and Child, I doubt that his mother stopped kissing him! Only two people – the woman who wet his feet with her tears, and kissed them, and anointed them with ointment – that woman, and Judas Iscariot. Of the woman who did not cease to kiss his feet, Jesus said, to Simon the Pharisee, that her sins, which were many, were forgiven 'for she loved much' and added 'He who is forgiven little, loves little.' To Judas, Jesus said: 'Would you betray the Son of Man with a kiss?'

I have looked at a large number of representations of the Passion and noted especially, among the soldiers and those bearing lanterns come to arrest Jesus, Judas – Judas embracing Jesus, Judas planting the kiss. The sign of affection, of reverence, of love, becomes the sign of betrayal, of broken trust. Again the words of the psalmist were fulfilled: 'Even my bosom friend in whom I trusted, who ate my bread, has lifted his heel against me', and again,

My heart is disquieted within me and the fear of death has fallen upon me. Fearfulness and trembling are come upon me and an horrible dread hath overwhelmed me... Wickedness is therein: deceit and guile go not out of their streets. For it is not an open enemy, that hath done me this dishonour, for then I could have borne it. Neither was it mine adversary, that did magnify himself against me, for then I would have hid myself from him. But it was even thou, my companion, my guide, and mine own familiar friend.

Sweet converse they had had hitherto; they had walked in fellowship within God's house.

This is not just a detail in the story of the Passion. It is not just an aspect of little consequence. It was not that the soldiers came suddenly to seize Jesus. It was not a kidnap. It was a betrayal and the memory of that act is renewed at every Eucharist, even in the midst of Easter joy, when the priest says 'who, on the same night in which he was betrayed'. Betrayal is of no consequence to those outside the household of faith, outside the Holy People; it means nothing to those who are not called friends by Jesus, but it means something to us.

It is easy to demonize Judas. The Gospels do it, speaking of Satan entering him, hiding his reasons, calling him a fraudster, embezzler and thief. Jesus is more matter-of-fact, sorrowful even, when he recognizes that betrayal is inevitable, necessary, and that someone has to do it but woe to that person by whom the Son of Man is betrayed. But what if Judas thought he was right, thought this was the best thing to do, believed that this would bring decisive action by Jesus? And was his betrayal worse, qualitatively speaking, than Peter's denial, than the fearfulness and flight of the others?

I wonder how Jesus felt as he washed Judas's feet, as he shared the meal with Judas, as he gave him the broken bread and passed him the cup. I wonder what weight of grief oppressed him in the matters concerning Judas Iscariot.

TUESDAY OF THE SEVENTH WEEK
OF EASTER
Joseph Barsabbas called Justus

In one of his ghost stories M. R. James has a character who does not appear in the story and so is not given a name. Joseph Barsabbas called Justus would hardly need his name because his sole appearance is as the disciple of Jesus, in Acts 1.23–6, who was not chosen to succeed to Judas's place among the apostles. He was put forward by the company as one of two candidates who fulfilled Peter's requirement that they should have accompanied the other apostles 'during all the time that the Lord Jesus went in and out among us, beginning from the baptism of John until the day when he was taken up from us'. We may feel that Joseph Justus's rejection is rather unfair. We know nothing of why Matthias was chosen and not Justus or why, given that Paul would later be called an apostle, it was not then possible to have more than twelve. The strongest reason is that Jesus himself called twelve and only Jesus could increase the number. We are, nevertheless, left with the difficulty that if some are called, then some others are clearly not called. It is a difficulty we face when someone who believes that they have a vocation and are called to a particular ministry finds that the Church does not affirm that vocation. There is a sense of being rejected.

It has often been observed that if the Twelve had been subjected to the methods that the Church now employs – selection panels, interviews, personal references and psychological testing – they would not have found a place beside Jesus. Others, looking at the clergy who have been accepted, wonder why they were chosen and the others were rejected, and those who have been through selection procedures and been affirmed are often dismayed that others who were with them were not selected. Those responsible for selection try to set the criteria out clearly and explain that 'not being recommended' for ordination training is not the same as being rejected. It is clear, however, that if you had a well-documented history of denying Christ or had been instrumental in persecuting the Church with the employment of pretty dubious methods leading to imprisonment and martyrdom, you would not today find a place among the clergy no matter how strong your subsequent sense of vocation.

Joseph Justus was rejected and we hear no more of him. He was one of the 120, and perhaps, as a later tradition testifies, he was one of the 70 sent out two by two to prepare for Jesus' itinerant ministry. Perhaps he gave up; perhaps he continued his ministry in the growing Church. I hope it was the latter and I think it was, though I have no evidence of it. I hope that he is one of those that we remember and celebrate on the feast of All Saints. He can represent for us those who were faithful to Christ even if they sought, and did not receive, strong affirmation or high office from the Church. Without them there is no Church. And one of the greatest sadnesses is that there are so many people – ordained and lay, formerly serving as clergy, readers, churchwardens – who no longer find a place in the Church, who, feeling rejected or used or burnt-out, have simply given up. They need a saint to be an example for them because it takes great strength and courage in such circumstances to stay with and in the Church and to go on doing what one is able to do, humbly and without recognition. Joseph Justus would be just such a saint.

WEDNESDAY OF THE SEVENTH WEEK
OF EASTER
I am Alpha and Omega

Before we reach Pentecost, I want to think about time. It is a strange experience for us to pass from one century to another and to find the nineteenth century, once so near at hand – my grandmother was born in the 1890s – now pushed far into the distance. And then having lived for nearly 50 years in the twentieth century I find myself propelled into what seemed in my childhood like the distant future, the twenty-first century. The lections of the Easter period keep us in three time zones at once. There is the Gospel telling us of the disciples' encounters with their risen Lord. There is Acts with its narrative of how those same disciples lived out their experience of the resurrection, how they preached and taught and healed in the name of the one who, being crucified, was yet alive. And the sprinkling of readings from the Revelation and some of the readings from Paul introduce an eschatological dimension, pointing us to the end-time. These readings show us the working-out of Jesus' resurrection and glorification; they show us the risen and re-ascended Lord, and remind us of the words said at the blessing of the Paschal Candle: 'Christ yesterday and today, the beginning and the ending, Alpha and Omega, all times belong to him and all the ages, to him be glory and power through every age for ever. Amen.'

To these three time zones we must add a fourth: ours. We do not merely hear these accounts of what went on in the past or is hoped for in the future. The word of God is addressed to us where we are. We hear in faith and as members of the community of faith. We are baptized into Christ's death and into his resurrection and we also are living out the experience of the resurrection. We are those of whom Jesus spoke to Thomas, those who are blessed because they believe even though they are not able, like him, to see the one in whom they believe.

These time zones give Christianity a particular character which differentiates it from other ways of looking at the world. First, the past is important. The key word is *tradition*. It signifies the act of handing on the faith from one generation. As St Paul said of the Eucharist, 'I have received from the Lord that which I also delivered unto you.' Our own word 'tradition' does not catch the full meaning of this. Tradition does not rest on us like a dead hand, it is a living and active process. And this handing-on is not like inheritance in which you receive from your father what he received from his grandfather and his great-grandfather before him. We can and do receive the faith directly from Scripture, hearing Jesus' own words and first-hand accounts of his life, and we also receive them as they have been received and understood through countless generations. The past is important. In some respects it is normative, but Christianity is not just about the past.

Second, the future is important. 'We look for the resurrection of the dead and the life of the world to come.' We may be less future-oriented than previous Christian ages. We find it harder to visualize the glory of Christ. The language of monarchy, of thrones and crowns, is harder for us now that our governments, monarchs and presidents are more like ordinary people. We cannot really imagine Jesus in a lounge suit behind a desk. But if we put him in a glorious robe, we somehow find ourselves all wearing the night-shirt of cartoons with angels, clouds and harps. We must not allow this difficulty to limit the future dimension. But we must acknowledge that the future is an area of uncertainty and the language and images we use to describe it will inevitably be imaginative, creative and even mythical. We are not called to live in the past nor to dwell only on the concerns of the present. As followers of Christ we are to look forward to the fulfilment of the promises of Christ, to the full expression of the Kingdom of God.

Between the two and strongly influenced by both is the present. Our faith is shaped by the past and has its ultimate direction in the future. We believe in Christ, crucified and risen. We look for the coming of the Kingdom. We live in the time between. Most of our concerns come from our present life. It is here that we have to fulfil our responsibilities. And the need to care for children, to find work, to pay bills, and so on, is not figurative or imaginary but very real. But it is not the fullness of reality. It does not contain all that is real and significant. And, in the name of Christ, crucified and risen, we must be prepared to challenge some of the absolutes of the present age, for as Christians we see the world differently, set between Alpha and Omega, between the beginning and the ending, between the empty tomb and Christ in the glory of the Father.

THURSDAY OF THE SEVENTH WEEK
OF EASTER
I will not leave you comfortless

Magdalena abducted the priest from the altar, bundled him into the motorcycle side-car and, in due course, tied him, still vested, to a tree. She wanted one thing – to be listened to in silence, without interruption. She had a confession to make and she wanted to be heard. She was tired of being cut short, of the flow of her speech being interrupted, and had an active contempt for all those people who, she claimed, specialized in the sabotage of evenly flowing thoughts, distracters, interrupters, signal-jammers, whisperers, know-alls, interveners, spoke-in-the-wheelers. Within this category came parents and other blood relations, teachers of all sorts, and all manner of psychologists, psychoanalysts, psychotherapists and others supposedly in charge of the welfare of people's souls. Magdalena took the precaution of gagging the priest. She ultimately wanted just one sentence from him: *Ego te absolvo*. The process of interruption began early: her mother did it in the middle of her second sentence, usually saying 'Don't talk nonsense.' Her father closed the door of his study, mumbling about a complicated child. The teacher became impatient and spoke of hurrying off to the fourth form. And of priests – well, she had sat in front of Burgundian, Austrian, Bavarian, Sicilian and Tyrolean priests and had never been allowed to deliver the whole of her, admittedly lengthy, confession. One – I can understand this – even fell asleep. He was English.

Now I hesitate to recommend books to people because they might be disappointed by them, and hold me responsible, or be shocked by them, and hold me responsible. *Magdalena the Sinner*, by Lilian Faschinger, translated from the German, was recommended to me by someone else on the strength, I think, of the opening line: 'And now you will listen to me, Reverend Father.' I in turn commend it to you as a good read, but you are not to hold me responsible if you are shocked.

My reading, of novels and essays as well as of theology, spirituality and both religious and secular history, is intended in part for entertainment and in part to inform and shape my exposition of Scripture in writing and preaching, my not-uncritical commendation of Christian faith and practice. Christianity is a faith rooted in history, expressed in and through the culture of the peoples who received the good news of God's saving work in Christ. That expression need not be, often isn't, positive. We find nothing positive in the sexual abuse of seminarians by a seminary rector who went on to be an archbishop and a cardinal, in the merciless beating of orphans by religious sisters, in paedophile priests or those clergy who, exploiting the power inherent in their office, have violated the vows of nuns. I can't imagine that we see anything that is positive in genocide, torture and burnings administered in the name of the Church. But there are also less dramatic wrongs, failures in guidance, in pastoral care, in fellowship, in brotherly and sisterly love, failures caused by frailty, tiredness, impatience, understandable error, as well as by hubris, callousness, personal ambition, dogmatism.

I could not help reading Magdalena's account of the way in which her discourse was interrupted without recalling the occasions when I haven't listened, when I have wanted to put off the person who asked to talk, when I have looked through them or beyond them to someone I needed to see or wanted to see, when I have been too busy or too tired. And one can hardly fail to think of times when one has been on the other side – wanting to speak and unable to. There is another book I read a few years ago. I, alas, remember nothing of the book, except its striking title: *Taking Care: An Alternative to Therapy*.

As the Church is depicted in literature we frequently see its negative aspects; the degree to which it fails to represent its founder's best intentions. We see the failures, the disappointment of legitimate hopes, the ones who went away, shook the ecclesiastical dust from their feet, pleaded that this was not what they wanted, not what they signed up for.

The post-resurrection, post-ascension Church faced – and still faces - a challenge: going on alone. Jesus says, 'I am with you always,' and promises the Spirit, and we believe him and know his presence in word and sacraments, but it is not, of course, the same as having him there. There will be those times when we check what we are doing against the Word of God in Scripture and find that we are off target, failing in our mission and ministry. We will fail because we are imperfect, fallible, because we tire and become irritable and cannot be happy, loving and caring all the time. And the odd, extraordinary, infuriating thing is that God seems to grasp us in our failures and to enable us to minister out of weakness, and often seems unaware of and unwilling to use our strengths. History teaches us that failure and disappointment are a real part of the life of the Church, but they are only a part.

It does not mean that we should somehow think they do not count or that we can pass over them in silence, without apology or explanation. We should strive, by God's grace and in God's strength, for a ministry, ordained and lay, that takes care, and a first step is to listen attentively, first to God, and then to those who come with their stories, their confessions and their needs to the Church as the body of Christ, the making present of his mission and saving work.

FRIDAY OF THE SEVENTH WEEK
OF EASTER
Faithful Cross above all other

It is not only Christ who is glorified in the liturgy. The liturgical calendar includes a significant feast day known as Holy Cross Day; it is observed not in Eastertide but on 14 September. The occasion of the feast was the finding of the True Cross and the subsequent consecration of Constantine's Basilica of the Holy Sepulchre in Jerusalem. It was, apparently, the Empress Helena, Constantine's mother, who found the Cross on 14 September 320. Eventually the 'finding' came to be celebrated in May, and on 3 May in the calendar of the Book of Common Prayer you will find the feast of the Invention of the cross; 'invention' here means 'discovery'. Then 14 September came to be observed as a celebration of the return to Jerusalem of the relic of the Cross stolen by the Persian king Chosroës. It was recovered in 628 by the Emperor Heraclius. In this way the occasion of the feast changed, something that is not unusual in the history of the liturgy. The hymns of Venantius Fortunatus in praise of the Cross were written for the entry of the relic of the True Cross into St Radegunde's monastery at Poitiers:

> Faithful Cross, above all other,
> One and only noble Tree,
> None in foliage, none in blossom,
> None in fruit thy peer may be;
> Sweet the wood, and sweet the iron,
> And thy load, most sweet is he.

A feast always celebrates something more than an historical (or possibly legendary) event. It also celebrates a mystery. The mystery here celebrated did not change: the Church glorifies the Cross of Christ with fullest love and enthusiasm as the sign of redemption. Christ was ultimately glorified through the Cross and so the Cross itself came to be glorified. One of the collects tells that Christ 'went not up to joy but first he suffered pain and entered not into glory before he was crucified'. At its most simplistic, this reminder might be no more than an exhortation to do the work before claiming the prize, to accept suffering because it leads to something better. Christianity has sometimes gone in for pious platitudes, but the Cross cannot be reduced to this. Not all suffering is beneficial – much of it destroys human life and dignity. The Cross points to a particular instance of redemptive suffering, of the triumph, under God, of the righteous man, and it gives that particular instance a universal significance. Jesus draws all people to himself as he is lifted on the Cross; he consecrates suffering, especially and uniquely the suffering of the innocent. Yet the pain, the humiliation and the sorrow remain. They are not magically removed. They remain but are consecrated, transformed and directed. Death can also be victory and need not be feared.

This transformation is akin to that which affects the Cross. The instrument of torture and painful death is made of wood that is cast away, cut down as unfruitful, thrown out as unusable. It has no beauty, it is ignoble, it is set in the place of death. After use, bloodstained and torn by nails, it is fit for nothing. But the wood on which the Saviour dies has dignity conferred upon it. It is no longer worthless but precious; no longer unfruitful but bearing the fruits of the Passion; no longer ignoble but sublime, adorning the crowns of kings, the foreheads of emperors. Its foliage and blossom are praised by the poet. It still bears the mark of the nails; it is still stained with blood, but it has become both the cross of sacrifice and the sign of victory – not, however, the latter without the former.

SATURDAY OF THE SEVENTH WEEK
OF EASTER
And Mary the mother of Jesus

Luke gives us the names of the eleven disciples who had been present at the ascension and who returned to the upper room in Jerusalem. There was Peter first, with the brothers, Zebedee's sons, John and James, the little group that Jesus often took off with him, and then Andrew, Simon Peter's brother, and Philip and Thomas the doubter, and Bartholomew, of whom nothing is known, and Matthew the tax-gatherer, and James the son of Alphaeus, and Simon, called the Zealot because of his adherence to the party that sought to overthrow Roman rule, and Judas the son of James. And these eleven devoted themselves to prayer, along with the women who had been so faithful in their friendship for and service of Jesus, and Jesus' brethren, and Mary the mother of Jesus.

Saturday is traditionally Mary's day, so I want to turn away from the anticipation of Pentecost for a moment to consider her. There are two good reasons for this. The first is the attractiveness of Mary. The second is the way in which the correct doctrine of Mary guarantees a correct doctrine of the incarnation. This is not, however, without its difficulties.

Women have not always been attractive to Christians, or perhaps I should say that women have been *too* attractive to male Christians. Although the general view of women in Western Christendom had softened by the fourteenth century, the view of monks and canons changed more slowly. From their viewpoint women were daughters of Eve and by that descent still primarily responsible for man's fall. As the medieval play of Adam and Eve put it, when Adam himself speaks:

> Oh, evil woman, full of treason . . .
> Forever contrary to reason,
> Bringing no man good in any season:
> Our children's children to the end of time
> Will feel the cruel whiplash of your crime.

The characteristic vice of women, as depicted in medieval Last Judgements, where men and women suffered eternal torments, was Unchastity; the characteristic vice of men, Pride or Avarice. I wonder how we would see it today!

But Mary was attractive in a different, a non-threatening way, attractive even to those in the forefront of the monkish execration of women, the Cistercians. Bernard of Clairvaux saw that our salvation, the recovery of our innocence, and our victory over our enemy depended on Mary's strength. Mary was the remaking of Eve; indeed, the angel's 'Ave' to Mary was seen as a deliberate reversal of the name 'Eva'.

> That angel who greets you with 'Ave'
> Reverses sinful Eva's name.
> Lead us back, O holy Virgin,
> Whence the falling sinner came.

The ordinary woman, caught somewhere between Eve and Mary, was uncompromisingly associated with the former, while the latter was held up as a model.

Nevertheless, Mary offered an attractiveness that drew men and women to her as, from the end of the eleventh century, devotion to the Virgin Mother grew in the West. God the Father seemed very remote. God the Son appeared as the all-just judge of the quick and the dead, and Mary appeared as the mother of mercy, gathering sinners beneath her cloak. Mary was accessible, and whether it was Marian devotion or other social and political factors, the Church's appreciation of women changed – not dramatically, but subtly, and the Church, which had always upheld the equality of women in marriage, came to see them as generally less threatening.

We are no longer caught up in that Eve–Mary dichotomy. Nor must we be drawn into Reformation argument about Mary's role; it belongs to a different age. We do not worship Mary, and Roman Catholics, no matter what the excesses of earlier ages and other cultures, have never done so. But in a faith that can sometimes seem too masculine, too patriarchal, she recalls us to the values of a gentleness that does not lack strength, of a love that endures all things, of a compassion that embraces men and women in their erring and straying, that would win them by love and not by fear. She shows a mother's deep love for her son that knows no limits and no barriers.

If Christ of old seemed too glorious, too mighty, robed in splendour, Mary was the means of approaching him. Today perhaps our Christ is all too limited, and we too familiar with him, lacking awe at his presence, evaluating his teaching as if it was the thought of some philosopher, the manifesto of some politician. Distance might be better; fear and trembling more appropriate, together with a simple, sweet devotion to her who said 'Behold, the handmaid of the Lord; be it unto me according to thy word.'

During Passiontide the Church considers how Mary shared inwardly and deeply in her son's sufferings as she met him on the way to the place of crucifixion and how she too made her way to Calvary and came to stand at the foot of the Cross. The mother of Jesus could not deny her heart; though she hated to see him suffer, she gazed with loving eyes upon those wounds of her son, those wounds by which, she knew, all men and women would be redeemed. Throughout Eastertide the liturgy, aware of her suffering, calls upon her to rejoice: Rejoice and be glad, O Virgin Mary, alleluia! For the Lord is truly risen, alleluia!

PENTECOST
When the day of Pentecost was fully come

Reaching the day of Pentecost I found that I stared for rather longer than usual at the blank space on the computer screen. It was not that I had nothing to say about the Holy Spirit of God. Quite the contrary. The Christian experience of the Spirit is so rich, so complex, that the difficulty is to know where to begin. The Spirit is the Lord, the giver of life, and to ask about the source of life is to ask about God, to face again the question of the divinely incomprehensible. This does not mean that we cannot talk about God but only that our knowledge of God is limited to what God reveals to us, to our experience of the divine nature. What then can we say of the Holy Spirit?

In baptism and confirmation we have all received the Spirit and the Spirit's manifold gifts, and the Spirit, once kindled within us, continues to grow. It does not destroy what we are, replacing it with something radically different; it is rather the case that the Spirit perfects us, working, if we will allow it, in each part of us. This is rather different from what might be expected. Contemporary television abounds in game shows in which competitors struggle to win money or else to get the material things they think they want. We might ask whether today's Church should not be able to guarantee well-being, a home, money, good food, foreign travel in exotic parts, visible success, other people's esteem, comfort, peace and security. And what do we get instead? We get the restlessness that the Spirit generates. He makes us restless with our possessions, our comfort, our respect. He is a tempest, blowing through, unsettling us, refusing us peace until we rest in God. The Spirit unsettles each of us in the way most fitting for us. No part of our life is exempt from his touch. Stage by stage, if we will, the Spirit moves us towards perfection in Christ.

Our will is important. The Spirit does not impose. Our free response is sought and elicited. We can frustrate the Spirit. We can deny his power. We do so when we are immobilized by choice, torn between two things, uncertain which way to go. As a basic rule we can be sure that the easy way is not the Spirit's way. Discipleship is costly. But when we turn to the Spirit, giving the divine will free rein in our lives, what happens then? St Francis shows us the way: perfect joy, he says, is not to be found in miracle or in prophecy or in knowledge, but in accepting and bearing the sufferings of Christ patiently for love of him. Now we may shrink from that but God chooses us because we are capable of whatever we are called to do. To refuse God, because of fear, doubt or even humility, is to be ungrateful, for the Spirit is a gift promised by Jesus, the presence of God in our lives. In other words we are invited into a deep relationship with God and the medium of that relationship is the Spirit. But no one in the Church has a monopoly on the Spirit and there is no single uniform way by which he works in our lives or is made manifest in the Church.

MONDAY AFTER PENTECOST
The light of thy Holy Spirit

The liturgy of the day of Pentecost, our old Whitsunday, reminds us of the great need that we have for the Holy Spirit of God. The Church has become increasingly aware of it during the last fifty or sixty years, but there has been a growing concentration on the more unusual gifts of the Spirit – on healings, slayings, inspired laughter, speaking in tongues and prophesyings – and there has been a tendency to bring some of them into worship. As vestments, incense and an abundance of candles have been a clear mark of a traditional catholic approach to worship, so the overhead projector, the music group with its keyboard, guitars and tambourines, the clapping, the raised hands, are distinctive marks of charismatic worship. We must be very careful not to confuse our tastes and our personal preferences with objective statements about the content of faith and worship. I may not like 'bells and smells' but this is not a good reason to reject the catholic understanding of the worship of the transcendent deity. I may not like 'happy clappy' worship but this is not a good reason to turn my back on the abundant gifts of the Holy Spirit.

The liturgy of the historic Roman Church had a remarkable simplicity and sobriety. It was marked by Roman gravity. Its exuberance comes later, the product of Bernini's Rome. The English liturgy comes from the Roman liturgy earlier in its life, during the Renaissance but before Baroque and, at its best, it retains a good deal of that gravity and sobriety, economy in words and simplicity in ceremonial. At times it has perhaps become too economical and too simple.

Archbishop Cranmer used the collect of the Roman Mass for Pentecost and it has continued in use in the new *Common Worship* of the Church of England. The collect points to three features of the pentecostal gift. First, the Holy Spirit brings light. Actually the opening line presents us with a few problems: 'God, who as at this time didst teach the hearts of thy faithful people, by the sending to them the light of thy Holy Spirit.' It uses language expressive of a different understanding of learning or of being taught from the one in common use. It places the focus on the heart. This is no longer a way in which we express ourselves. We do, however, know what it means. When the disciples on the road to Emmaus say 'Did not our hearts burn within us?' we understand them. We might say we felt excited, moved by what we heard, but we understand them as we might a foreign or archaic language, and we might also have had an experience that equates with theirs. After all, we say 'I see what you mean', and that indicates understanding, a moment of grasping what someone else is saying. Much of what I have written here has also involved figurative use of language. The Holy Spirit illuminates our darkness, clarifies our understanding, teaches us what is needful.

Second, the Spirit is able to give us a right judgement. This is a crucial gift as knowledge moves into action: the ability to discern what is right and to act upon it. Notice that there is nothing extraordinary or supernatural about this vital gift. It doesn't involve speaking in tongues or prophesying. It reinforces the teaching that grace perfects our nature. There isn't another new layer that is made up of distinctive Christian activities. The Spirit is addressed to us where we are, in our real needs, making complex decisions, caught in a game of choices where right judgement is crucial.

Third, the Spirit comforts or consoles, and this is a source of joy. Consolation, according to Dr Johnson's dictionary, is that which frees us from the sense of misery. Comfort originally means what strengthens, encourages, supports and invigorates and not, as in the current sense, to soothe in grief or trouble. Cranmer's 'holy comfort' is divine strength, a renewal of our powers as the Spirit makes of us a new creation. And it also consoles, for it lifts us above the misery of contemplating, as the psalmist says, the shortness and futility of life. The Spirit gives us purpose, direction and hope, and gives us joy in believing.

The liturgy sees us remade by the power of the Spirit in baptism and confirmation, in the Eucharist and in the other sacraments. It sees the Spirit at work in the Church and active in our lives when we accept spiritual gifts. It does not imagine us secluded in a Christian ghetto. Cranmer abandoned postcommunion prayers. That given in the old Roman Missal for today dates from the ninth century. Its language is a little too florid to be Roman and it was probably written in a German monastery, but it surely expresses our need: 'May our hearts be cleansed by the infusion of the Holy Spirit, Lord, and may our souls grow fertile under the dew he sheds upon them.'

TUESDAY AFTER PENTECOST
And Peter lifted up his voice

Peter really did tend the flock entrusted to him. The Acts of the Apostles practically begins with Peter addressing the inhabitants of Jerusalem but it tells us nothing of what happened to him, except that strong intimation in the Gospel of the death that would come to him. The tradition, as set down in the Golden Legend, says that Peter went to Rome in the fourth year of the reign of Claudius and dwelt there 25 years. Towards the end Paul was sent to join him.

Pope Leo the Great preached on the feast of the apostles Peter and Paul when he was Bishop of Rome in the fifth century. He explained that it was by the providence of God that the Roman Empire grew, that the Gospel might spread with it, even though those responsible for its advance did not themselves know the reason. Peter, chief of the apostolic band, was sent to Rome because it was *caput mundi*, head of the world. Leo said:

What nation had not representatives then living in this city; or what peoples did not know what Rome had learnt? Here it was that the tenets of philosophy must be crushed, here that the follies of earthly wisdom must be dispelled, here that the cult of demons must be refuted, here that the blasphemy of all idolatries must be rooted out, here where the most persistent superstition had gathered together all the various errors which had anywhere been devised.

And Leo points out that Peter, who had once been frightened by the high priest's maid in the courtyard of Caiaphas's house, was now rooted in his love of Christ and feared nothing as he witnessed to Christ in Rome.

The story is told that Peter and Paul again encountered the magician Simon Magus, who appears in the Acts, and defeated him, though he was a favourite of Nero's. The apostles were imprisoned but soldiers, converted by Peter's preaching, released them and Peter was urged to leave the city. When he, reluctantly, passed outside the city gates, he saw Christ coming towards him and said: *Domine, quo vadis?* 'Whither goest thou, Lord?' Jesus replied: 'I am going to Rome to be crucified anew.' 'To be crucified again,' said Peter. 'Yes,' said Christ, and Peter said he would go and be crucified with him. The Lord departed but Peter returned to the city to face martyrdom. Peter, an alien, was condemned to be crucified. Paul, a Roman citizen, was condemned to be beheaded. They died on the same day – 29 June – at the same hour but not at the same place. Peter objected that he was not worthy to be crucified as the Lord was, and he was turned upside-down. Peter's disciples arranged for the burial of his body, but in later years his bones became confused with those of Paul. One account says that Pope Silvester weighed the bones and divided them into equal portions, half to the church of St Paul outside the walls and the other to St Peter's on the Vatican Hill.

Leo pointed to Nero's madness which made him the first to unleash a general persecution against the Church. He could not grasp the way in which God's grace was increased by this. As the Psalmist says: 'Precious in the eyes of the Lord is the death of his saints.' Persecution does not diminish but increases the Church; it is nourished by the blood of the martyrs, and Rome knew many thousands of martyrs after the apostles. Peter and Paul were indivisible and invincible in death. Leo concluded his sermon like this:

> And over this band of martyrs, dearly beloved, set forth by God as an example of patience and in order that we might be confirmed in the faith, there must be rejoicing everywhere, but especially for these two who have been raised to so high a place in the Church that they are like the twin light of the eyes within the body whose head is Christ. About their merits and virtues, which exceed our power of speech, we must make no distinction, for they are equal in election, united in their toils, undivided in their death. And we are clear, beloved, and firmly believe that among the toils and troubles of this life we must always be assisted in obtaining God's mercy by the prayers of these special interceders, that we may be raised by the Apostles' merits in proportion as we are weighed down by our own sins.

WEDNESDAY AFTER PENTECOST
To hear the apostles teach

The Acts of the Apostles says that, after Pentecost, the Christians 'met constantly to hear the apostles teach, and to share the common life, to break bread and to pray.' We see five particular features. The first was that they met constantly. They were a genuine community. They knew one another, even though their numbers were increasing rapidly. They spent time together and were so close that Luke is able to speak of them being 'of one mind'. They didn't just meet to be sociable. Primarily they met to hear the teaching of the apostles, so that they might be nurtured in their new-found faith. They were willing to learn and they had ready teachers. They also shared a common life. They met in their homes, they went daily to the Temple, they shared meals, and all they did was marked by unfeigned joy. That doesn't mean that they never disagreed about anything. It means that the joy that they had in their salvation was greater than the sadness caused by dissent or disagreement.

They also gathered to break bread. This is the earliest name given to the Eucharist for, as we noted earlier, Christ was made known to the disciples at Emmaus in the breaking of bread, and it was precisely this action that he had commanded them to do 'in memory of me'. So they met together as a community to proclaim by this simple act the death of the Lord until he should come again. They also met to pray, and this line implies that most of their prayer was corporate. It was not a personal activity that you could do just as well by yourself. It was something done by and with the community of faith.

They met constantly to hear the apostles teach, and to share the common life, to break bread and to pray: what was the result of this? First, there was a sense of awe everywhere; a sense of amazement, excitement and anticipation. The Lord was working great things and through the ministry of the apostles many marvels and signs were brought about. Second, the Lord added to their number those whom he was saving, and he did it *day by day*.

This then is the model, the example of the Church of the apostles. We have much to learn from it. Sunday by Sunday we affirm that we believe in and belong to a Church which is one, holy and catholic, and that it is also apostolic. We too follow in the footsteps of the apostles and receive their teaching.

THURSDAY AFTER PENTECOST
And the Lord added to their number

Peter, filled with the Holy Spirit, was prepared to boast of what God had done, and he who once denied his Lord now proclaimed his faith without fear. I wonder if we ever find ourselves inclined to boast of our Christian faith and of our membership of the Christian Church? Do we ever find ourselves saying, 'I am a Christian' or 'I am a member of the Church of England' with pride? I think it unlikely. The frank admission of Christian faith all too often gets a negative response. It suggests, perhaps, that you are going to embark on a bit of evangelization, on an attempt to convert. By contrast, if you say 'I go to St George's' – that statement is largely unthreatening. It speaks of a personal preference rather than a strongly held conviction. At most you might be going to ask for a contribution to the building fund!

If I am right, then this is something to be regretted – our loss of pride in being Christian, in being redeemed. What is needed is an apology – not frank acknowledgement of an offence given together with an explanation that it was not intended and regret for having caused it, but a robust defence of the position being held, a vindication from accusation or aspersion. We need to be ready and able to make such an apology for our Christian faith and practice and that means, of course, that we must understand thoroughly the objections to Christian belief and we must argue our case.

All too often we are caught on the hop. We are unable to rebut quickly and effectively the trite and insubstantial attacks made on Christianity. For example, the constant repetition of the line 'You do not have to go to church in order to be a Christian' does not make it true. We know that it is possible to believe the Gospel without going to church. We know that it is possible to pray and to worship God at all times and in all places, but we also know that Christianity as such begins with Christ calling disciples. We cannot fulfil the basic commandments of Jesus – to evangelize, to baptize, to celebrate the memorial meal and to love one another as he loves us – in isolation. Adherence to the community of faith and attention to apostolic teaching is an essential, non-negotiable part of Christianity. We know this but we find it hard to express, to present it and argue it in a persuasive way and so to help people overcome some of the difficulties they may experience in belonging to such a community.

The Bible offers three approaches to witness in an environment that is potentially or really hostile. Each approach, we might say, anticipates rejection. The first frankly acknowledges it. It is that of the prophet Ezekiel. Those to whom the prophet is sent are a nation of rebels, impudent and stubborn. The prophet has to make known the Lord's words whether the people hear or refuse to hear. Do not be afraid, he is told – do not be afraid of their words, do not be dismayed by their looks – press on and speak my words to them. God tells the prophet that, though the people he addresses are hard-headed and stubborn, yet God will make him even harder-headed and even more stubborn. The point here is that we must not give up and we must not compromise. We must not dilute the Gospel in order that it might be more palatable.

The second approach is a modified version of the first. It comes from Paul. The apostle is only prepared to boast of the grace and mercy of God. His own elation is kept down by the thorn in the flesh. He recognizes his weakness and imperfection, but he offers as a word from the Lord an absolutely basic principle of ministry: 'My grace is sufficient for you, for power is made perfect in weakness.' It is not, then, that we are expected of ourselves to be mighty witnesses, though we are expected to be faithful witnesses. There is, however, a further expectation – that we will not flee in the face of insults, hardships, persecutions and calamities, but clinging the more closely to God in our weakness, we will find strength. Faithfulness in weakness. Steadfastness in witness. These are the features of this approach.

The third approach, found in the Gospels, is amazement. Even Jesus was amazed, amazed at the lack of faith of so many who heard him. We expect people to respond to the Gospel. We expect them to come to church – especially a lovely church full of friendly people. They don't. We are amazed. Are we downhearted? Well, perhaps, sometimes. But let us continue to be amazed, for our amazement suggests that we are so convinced of the attractiveness of Jesus Christ that we cannot possibly understand how anyone can turn away from him. Jesus was amazed – amazed that in his own home town people should question his authority and take offence at his words. We too should go on being amazed. We are bearing witness to the good news of human redemption, we are continuing the work of reconciliation – and we should be amazed when people do not want to hear, when they take offence, when they are offensive. What we must not do is give up.

We might learn something from our Christian history. It is clear from my reading of medieval monastic chronicles that our forebears in the faith saw the monastery as the expression and fulfilment of that vision of the apostolic Church given to us by Luke in the Acts of the Apostles. Those who entered the Church were fleeing from the world, saving themselves from corruption, devoting themselves to the apostolic teaching and fellowship, and sharing a common life, marked by the absence of personal property, for all things were held in common. Those who entered the monastery, whether in the enthusiasm of youth, or at the end of a long search, or at the conclusion of life, did so for very similar reasons. Whether in the first century or the twelfth century, Christians were persuaded that there was very little chance of salvation if one continued to live in the world, and the ideal was that of renouncing the world, the flesh and the devil.

The New Testament does not say that the apostolic Church was a perfect community, though it clearly aspired to faithfulness to the teaching of Christ. It had its arguments and its divisions. It had those who tried to retain their wealth and still be in the Church. As it grew, so it became more difficult to maintain purity of doctrine and of practice, and Paul soon finds himself correcting both the beliefs and the moral practice of the young churches. Peter reminds Christians that they are ransomed from the futile ways of their ancestors and that their trust is in God; their faith and hope are set on God, and that means that they must apply themselves to love one for another, to the nurturing of fellowship, the building up of the community of faith.

The monastic life was an experiment. It became more significant as urban life developed. These two, the monastery and the city, seemed to be at odds with each other. One represented flight from the world; the other was marked by a deep worldliness. The city was the place of trade, markets, money, status, of seeking personal and dynastic fortunes. The monastery, while not a stranger to trade and to rents, was centred on worship and prayer. Later developments in the religious life, notably the emergence of the Franciscans and Dominicans, with their great urban preaching churches, represented an attempt to bring together the monastery and the city. My own church, St Bartholomew's, was an Augustinian house; it seems to have been marked by fidelity in worship and in the care of the sick and poor as well as by a shrewd eye for business on the fairground and in the market.

The monastic experiment came to an end. Monasteries still exist, of course, but they hardly represent the cutting edge in terms of the Church's attitude to the world. There have been other experiments – Methodism, for example, on the Protestant side, was an approach to Christianity that attracted the growing middle classes, and the worker priest movement, on the Roman Catholic side, was a valiant attempt after the Second World War to recover for the Christian faith those whose lives were controlled by the factory hooter rather than the church bell.

Each experiment – and every century has seen many – represents an attempt to reconcile the biblical vision of the Church with the reality of living in the world. This need to find a way to live in the world without violating the most basic principles of our faith remains a pressing one; not least because that is the very minimum asked of us. The Gospel urges us to continue God's reconciling work, to promote justice and peace, to bring the good news of Jesus Christ to this generation, and to set our minds on things heavenly rather than things earthly. I believe that we begin to do this by holding before our own eyes a vision of something eternal, stable, tranquil and transcendent, a vision of something heavenly for which we strive, of a perfection that can be ours. I believe that we need to recover a sense of God as sovereign, and not amenable to manipulation, to psychological games. What we have to do is to come into a real relationship with the divine majesty marked as much by the recognition of the distance between creature and Creator as by faith, hope and love. So we begin from 'right worship' – in Greek, *orthodoxy* – in which, as we give glory and praise to God, we affirm that relationship. We do not become cosy with God but acknowledge God as Lord.

This was a most characteristic feature of the apostolic Church – they spent much time together in the Temple and they praised God. When we have got that right – when worship is central to our lives – then we are ready for further stages of development, for the increase of fellowship and the nurturing of love one for another. Worship is not flight from the world but, as the coming and going of the tide sweeps the beach and refreshes it, so our movement in and out of formal worship renews our lives and increases our ability to live faithfully in the world.

SATURDAY AFTER PENTECOST
Come, Holy Ghost, our souls inspire

This is our prayer as we continue to celebrate the outpouring of the Holy Spirit of God on the apostles on the first
Pentecost of the Church. This is our prayer but what do we
mean by it? What do we expect when we ask for a further
gift?

The Spirit of God may influence our lives even before
baptism, especially if we come to Christian faith in adulthood.
It then prepares the way, making it possible for us to affirm
our faith in and submission to Christ. At baptism, whether
as children or adults, we receive the Holy Spirit in the way
appropriate to our age, maturity and disposition. As the Holy
Spirit moved over the waters of creation, as it overshadowed
Mary at the annunciation, as it appeared at Christ's own baptism
in the Jordan, so the Spirit is present and active in baptism.
Remember, God does not overpower us, violating our own
will, but draws us to himself, eliciting our free response. His
grace perfects what is already there; it does not destroy it. The
Spirit ministers divine grace.

There is a new outpouring of the Spirit at confirmation.
You may remember how the bishop in confirmation recites
the manifold gifts of grace: the spirit of wisdom and understanding, the spirit of counsel and ghostly or inward strength;
the spirit of knowledge and true godliness; and the spirit of
holy fear. This is the list given in Isaiah 11 and it refers to the
one who comes forth from the root of Jesse – that is to say
the Messiah, the Christ. These are the qualities needed for
spiritual growth, and again the outpouring is appropriate to

age, maturity and disposition, to the ministries that are available. There is, as St Paul says, a diversity of gifts, but the same Spirit, a variety of service but the same Lord.

The Spirit is, therefore, indwelling. We receive the Spirit and the Spirit becomes part of us. There is no time after we profess the Christian faith or after baptism that the Spirit is absent from us. But we also freely use the language of the Spirit being sent – 'Send down thy Holy Spirit' we pray, or 'Give us the gifts of thy Holy Spirit.' We do not make these prayers because the Spirit is absent or we are devoid of gifts, but we ask that the Spirit should strengthen us for particular forms of service or ministry and that we should be remade and renewed. This renewal is particularly needed at the beginning of a decisively new work of grace taking place in our lives.

Because the Spirit is already within us, and if, by prayer and participation in worship and by reception of the sacraments, we have grown in awareness of the Spirit, then when new opportunities for service are presented to us we are ready to grasp them. We are schooled by the Spirit until we are ready. Then comes a moment of decision. If you read the *Spiritual Exercises* of St Ignatius Loyola, you will find that a major part of them is devoted to spiritual decision-making, to being certain that we are doing what God invites us to do and not doing so on the spur of the moment but after careful and, as we say, prayerful, consideration. And if like Moses called to be Israel's ambassador before Pharaoh or like Amos the son of the sycamore-dresser called to be a prophet or like the disciples of Christ called to justify their faith before the Jewish courts we plead our weakness and ignorance, our lack of verbal skill or intellectual ability, then God assures us that his strength is sufficient for us and the Spirit will give us utterance.

The school of Christian discipline urges us neither to be over-zealous in seeking out extraordinary ministries or high office in the Church nor to be over-reluctant in accepting that to which God undoubtedly calls us. We may never be called to do more than to live in such a way that we are pleasing to God, availing ourselves of the gifts of grace by which we are justified and counted worthy to stand in his presence and serve him. The Holy Spirit enables us to do this, and we do not necessarily have other gifts added to us – power to heal, to speak in tongues, to prophesy, and so on. But we may be called to witness to Christ in a more dynamic and public way; we may be called unexpectedly, as were the eleven, and given those gifts needed for the mission and ministry of the Church. By a renewed gift of the Spirit we may move into more ardent and more demanding love of God.

To pray 'Come, Holy Spirit' is to take a risk, but the risk is always worth taking.

TRINITY SUNDAY
O Trinity of blessed light

There was a major row in the twelfth century between the Benedictine Abbey of Cluny, in Burgundy, founded in 910, and the Cistercian Order, founded in 1098 in order to revive the primitive observance of the rule of St Benedict. Cluny had been ruled by a long succession of saintly abbots. It had flourished and grown in size and had engendered an enormous family of dependent priories all over Europe. Cluny was distinguished by its elaborate liturgy. The inexhaustible marvels of the Church's year were spread out before the eyes of faith in this sublime service of the King of Kings. The Cluniac vision was of unity between heaven and earth, a vision realized and expressed in an elaborately ordered liturgy. On the greatest feasts the choir floor was covered with carpets and the stalls and sanctuary hung with tapestries, a great number of candles were used and there were solemn processions. On Christmas Day and on Easter Day 493, candles burned in hanging chandeliers and five great candelabra burned around the altar. At Candlemas, twelve candelabra burned before the altar and five behind it, and all the community went in procession, bearing relics, holy water, censers and candlesticks, and singing.

The Cistercians rejected all this and looked for simplicity – in their faith, in their buildings and in their liturgy. St Bernard took exception to the immense height, immoderate length, superfluous width, the sumptuous splendour and the curious pictures of the third church of Cluny begun in 1089 and finished in 1132. The Cistercians berated the Cluniacs for their beautiful paintings, for beautiful and costly cloaks, for beautiful hanging tapestries of many colours, for beautiful and costly windows, for blue-coloured glass, for copes and chalices with golden orphreys and chalices of gold ornamented with precious stones. Necessity and utility, said the monk of Cîteaux, do not require all these things. The Cluniac asked, in response, what more becoming way was there to honour the most holy sacrament of Christ than to use these precious things?

You might guess where I would stand in the argument between Cluny and Cîteaux: I am a natural Cluniac. I believe passionately in the intersection of heaven and earth in the liturgy and the sacraments, though not only there, and I am committed to the idea that we should embellish the liturgy with all the artistic and musical skill, with all the wealth, and with all the ceremony we can command. But my reason for raising the issue here in our reflection on Trinity Sunday is not to offer an *apologia* for liturgy. In a medieval dialogue between a Cistercian and a Cluniac, the former objects that the Abbey of Cluny observes a feast of the Holy Trinity. The Trinity should have no special feast day, says the Cistercian, since we praise and venerate the Holy Trinity in hymns, psalms, responsories and masses every day when we say 'Glory be to the Father, Son, and Holy Spirit.'

In other words, the objection to the feast is that the Trinity is already praised and needs no extra veneration. This objection takes us to the heart of the feast. It is not an occasion for the preacher to discourse learnedly on the doctrine of the Holy Trinity. It is not an opportunity for erudite explanations. It is an occasion for worship – 'Early in the morning our song shall rise to thee'. It is the very rounding off and completion of the liturgical year. It is itself a great doxology, an offering of praise to the holy and undivided Trinity.

There have always been those who would deny the need for any feast and indeed for any sacrament. Their argument is simple. Take the Eucharist, the holy meal of the people of God. Some would argue that we do not need this sacramental meal, for every meal should be a celebration of God's love for us and of our communion with him and with each other. But human nature calls for something more, for a rhythm of the ordinary and the celebratory, for the punctuation of our life by those occasions that bring to the fore and express and reaffirm those things that are truly important for us, individually and personally, as a nation, and as a community of faith. Yes, perhaps every day we should celebrate the Trinity, and every meal should be a sacramental sharing, and for a few exceptional people this may be so, but the rest of us need our fasts and festivals, our sacred meals, and the cycle of celebrations of the mystery of our redemption.

The Cistercians did not prevail. From the Abbey of Cluny, Trinity Sunday spread throughout the Latin West. It was particularly popular in England because it was the day on which, in 1162, London's own saint, Thomas Becket, was consecrated bishop. I must also express a personal interest, for Trinity Sunday 1953 was my birthday. Both the Sarum Missal and the Book of Common Prayer reckoned the Sundays from the end of the liturgical commemorations of Christ's life as Sundays after Trinity. So it was until the *Alternative Service Book* changed it to Sundays after Pentecost, and *Common Worship* has now changed it back.

Trinity Sunday points us to a way of worship. Our prayer and praise is addressed to the Father, through the Son, in the power of the Holy Spirit. The Father is not God alone. The cartoon God, with a long white beard and a crown, sitting on a throne in heaven, is not the Trinitarian God. Our God is a unity of three persons. The nature of God as Trinity was set out in the Athanasian Creed in the Prayer Book. That creed, of great length and complexity, was recited at Morning Prayer on thirteen holy days throughout the year. It has largely disappeared now, but it was an attempt to set the Church's teaching into the context of worship.

It is as we offer praise to God that we are most aware of the Trinity. Yet the Trinity should also permeate our Christian lives because the great binding principle is love, and that love overflows like a fountain to drench the whole world. Worship brings us to the fountain's rim, brings us to the living water that we may drink and no more be thirsty, that we may wash and always be clean. We should come willingly to the source of all love and power and give glory to God, Father, Son and Holy Spirit.

MONDAY AFTER TRINITY SUNDAY
Believing, trusting and loving

Thomas à Kempis, fifteenth-century author of the celebrated spiritual classic *The Imitation of Christ*, gave a warning that is particularly apposite for those preparing to preach on Trinity Sunday. 'What gain is it', he said, 'for you to speak profoundly about the Trinity, if you are lacking in humility and so are displeasing to the Trinity?' Profound words make no one holy and just. A virtuous life makes you dear to God. Vanity of vanities, and all is vanity, except to love God and to serve him only. The whole school of spirituality to which à Kempis belonged – the *Devotio Moderna* – took an anti-intellectual stance. They were, I think, tired of learning without holiness, of sterile theological dispute that led nowhere and certainly not to the God who was its supposed object.

Their position represents one pole in the bipolarity of medieval Western Christianity. À Kempis's plea is for love of Jesus above all things. Let every other love be set aside, whether of other people, or knowledge, or possessions. The one who embraces Jesus shall be made strong for ever. Love him, keep him for your friend, for when all others desert you, he will not forsake you. Well and good. These are words we should heed. After faith, love is the most important characteristic of the Christian life. Second to faith in time, love is greater than faith, as the apostle Paul teaches us. We know from human relationships how closely related these are, believing in someone, trusting them, and loving them. Jesus says, 'You must believe me.' Then he says, 'If you love me keep my commandments.'

But there is another pole. Jesus asks Philip, Do you still, after all this time, not know me? And again, he speaks of the Spirit of truth whom the disciples know. Knowledge is the other pole. À Kempis quotes from the master of the men who know, Aristotle, the opening lines of the *Metaphysics*, words much quoted by another Thomas: 'All men naturally desire to know.' Against them he sets contempt for knowledge, which avails nothing without the fear of God. Cease from inordinate desire of knowing, he says, for therein is much distraction and deceit. But these two, love and knowledge, should not be set against each other, should not be placed in contradiction and opposition. They are two poles of a single whole. Medieval spirituality grew out of patristic spirituality that saw in the entire universe the imprint of God, which saw in human beings the image of God. The medieval synthesis, before it crumbled away, held together in perfect harmony the love of learning and the desire for God. These two were held together because of their common source. The Son and the Spirit proceed from knowledge and love. When in human life they are promoted together, then a strong and authentic spirituality emerges which nourishes both great mystics and great theologians. The Middle Ages, for a time, had both.

The truth of God that is revealed to us is beyond our understanding, and yet it invites reason to come to a measure of understanding, to enable us to give an account of the hope that is in us. The good news must be shared, and from within the tension between the all-surpassing truth and the need to communicate it comes our striving to understand: faith seeking understanding. This is the source of that discourse about God that we call theology. But in faith we also come to know the goodness of God, and begin to love God. Love ever desires to know the beloved better, and as we know him better, we love him more.

From whence does this unity come? From the image of God we carry, the image not only of the persons of the Trinity but also of their interrelation. Catherine of Siena, in the fourteenth century, expressed the nature of this image so well:

> You said, Let us make humankind in our image and like-ness. And this you did, eternal Trinity, willing that we should share all that you are, high eternal Trinity! You, eternal Father, gave us memory to hold your gifts and share your power. You gave us understanding so that, see-ing your goodness, we might share the wisdom of your only-begotten Son. And you gave us free will to love what our understanding sees and knows of your truth, and so share the mercy of your Holy Spirit.
>
> (*The Dialogue*)

This reflected Trinity is found in the writings of St Augustine. 'May I remember you,' he prayed. 'May I understand you and may I love you. Increase these gifts in me until you have re-formed me completely.'

There was a reason, then, for this speculation flowing into prayer; a logic for Augustine, for Catherine, for Richard of St-Victor and others who followed them in making the Trinity the heart of faith and spirituality – the logic of return, of the soul's yearning for that intimacy with the Trinity intended by God. A restlessness, Augustine calls it. Catherine, excited by the graces already received, speaks of the light that makes truth known, calls the Trinity craftsman and herself the handiwork, calls the Trinity a deep sea and longs to swim in it and explore it.

We could pause here, if space and time allowed, and explore for ourselves the theology of the Trinity that these spiritual guides set forth. It is a thing worth doing in itself. We could see how Augustine calls the Spirit love, and Richard calls him gift. The movement of return to God – our return – is initiated by the Word of God, who in receiving all in love from the Father returns all in love. The Spirit is that love, the gift within the Trinity, given to us to urge us to turn toward God in responsive love. We could go on and find that the strictly theological and the poetical are one, and the poetry is love poetry. And knowing that there were, and are, such guides, we must further ask how Thomas à Kempis came so to deprecate learning and to separate it from love. Were there so many whose lives were not answerable to their learning and who perished because they took little care of serving God? Truly, when the day of judgement comes, he says, we shall not be examined on what we have read but on what we have done; not how well we have spoken, but how religiously we have lived.

It gives the preacher, scholar and theologian pause for thought. And rightly so. And yet the Trinity is our model and our guide, and there, in the unity of Father, Son and Spirit, are held together wisdom and love. So we are to know God and to love him. And loving him, we must know him better, and witness in both love and knowledge to the glory of the eternal Trinity.

TUESDAY AFTER TRINITY SUNDAY
A vision of the moon

A number of strands shaped the life of the Church at any time and, as we approach the end of this series of reflections and meditations, we can, I think, identify four:

- first, the desire to worship God and to celebrate the sacraments in a fitting way, sometimes simple, sometimes elaborate;
- second, the reflections of theologians upon the content of Christian belief – this more or less systematic reflection does not take place in isolation, for theologians teach and preach and so new insights and understandings become widespread;
- third, devotion – that is to say, the factors that shape the religious affections of people, both the clergy and religious and lay people;
- the fourth factor might even be said to be the most significant; we may call it chance, accident or perhaps better providence. One devotion becomes popular and widely spread and another is limited to one monastery or one area; the reason for this may be simple – it may depend upon the influence of those who supported or came in contact with that devotion.

These four factors were at work in the emergence of the feast that concludes this cycle, the feast of thanksgiving for the body and blood of Christ, Corpus Christi. The human originator of the feast was one Juliana, a nun of Mont-Cornillon near Liège. The spirituality of her house was largely Cistercian, marked by simplicity, by asceticism, by a devotion to the humanity of Christ. Juliana was born in 1193 and took the habit in 1207. She had a particular fondness for the Eucharist and early showed a tendency towards rather extreme spiritual practices; it seems likely that she was a holy anorexic, craving spiritual rather than material food. Torn away from prayer in order to eat, Juliana told her nurse and her sisters that she wanted better and more beautiful food. In 1208 or 1209 she had a vision. Visions were frequent in the medieval Church and one was not necessarily taken seriously in recounting it. Juliana saw the Church symbolized by the full moon. The moon, because it has no light of its own but reflects the sun, is a frequent symbol for the Church. This full moon had one dark spot and a subsequent vision revealed that what was missing was a liturgical feast of Christ's body, Corpus Christi. Though in the years to come Juliana became prioress and established the celebration of such a feast in her house, it might just have stayed a local devotion if it had not been for the interest shown by various distinguished bishops and theologians. The Archdeacon of Liège, Jacques Pantaleon, was one such; in less than fifty years he would be pope and it was by his decree that the feast began the long process to universal observance, a process not completed until the latter years of the Avignon papacy in the fourteenth century.

Juliana's vision and the action that followed from it show how easily worship and devotion may be combined. At least it shows how easily they could be combined then. What has happened in our own day is a divorce between popular devotion and formal liturgy. We saw something like popular devotion in the aftermath of the death of the Princess of Wales. It was deeply rooted in traditional ideas of marking what is important with signs, with offerings, with vigils and with tears. The popular has largely been excluded from the more cerebral mainstream churches, partly, and quite deliberately, by the clergy, for popular devotion is hard to control, defies structure, is largely lay, and may easily pass the bounds of what is theologically acceptable. But when devotion and liturgy unite within a theological framework, well then anything is possible. In this case, two mystics, an unlettered monk, a bishop, a Dominican cardinal, two popes better known for their political skills than for their spirituality, and the greatest theologian of the thirteenth century succeeded in taking a primary mystical experience – Juliana's vision – and giving it a liturgical and devotional expression that has endured through seven centuries.

The seedbed of such growth was an extraordinary degree of religious practice – deep immersion in Scripture, daily prayer, fervent longing for union with Christ, fasting, meditation on Christ in his humanity, long hours spent in silent vigil aided by statues and paintings. Our spirituality would seem as impoverished to the medieval as our churches would seem colourless. Perhaps that is just a matter of style: as our houses are much less fussy than those of our Victorian and Edwardian forebears, so our churches are simpler and, although there is a new movement to enrich our worship, our liturgy too is simple and stripped down. There are times when it is necessary to peel away the layers and return to basic frameworks and structures, but there is also a moment to replenish, to return to older, more complex ideas and devotions. If what has gone before is not to our taste, we must develop what is new. The materials are all there, but for the moment our spirituality looks rather bare, modernistic, over-cerebral, lacking warmth and affection or else tending to drift into the saccharine and sentimental. We need to recapture the affective dimension, engaging the heart as well as the mind, and expressing in our worship, in the way in which our hearts and minds are correlated with our voices, some inner warmth, some longing for the love of Christ. The last few years have seen a renewed interest in spirituality but we have hardly gone from research and study, from reading about historic movements, to the construction and enrichment of our own profound spiritual practice. We do not have to wait for clerics and scholars. The lesson of history is that the laity on their knees, with their Bibles in their hands, with their eyes fixed on God, and their hearts full of longing, lead the way.

WEDNESDAY AFTER TRINITY SUNDAY
Hail! true Body

'Adoration,' said Dom Prosper Guéranger, Cécile Bruyère's mentor, 'is an act whereby we acknowledge our nothingness lovingly before God; we give to him what we have received from him; we declare and proclaim him to be worthy of all praise from all creatures.' 'Adore' is not in fact a word we often use, and though we might in pretty extreme circumstances tell another person that we adore them, it is a word that is primarily concerned with our relation to God. The *Shorter Oxford Dictionary* comes pretty close to Dom Prosper when it defines adore as 'to make an act of the mind and will in acknowledgement of the infinite perfection of God'.

Adoration is, therefore, an act involving mind and will. It is an act in which we affirm our smallness, our utter insignificance. But it is not a response to fear, to threat, to coercion. It is a response to love, to God's love for us and for the outpouring of that love in creation and redemption. In adoration we know ourselves as loved and know that all we have and all we are and all we will be comes from God. This is, of course, very different from our usual awareness of our own dignity, our own status, powers, abilities and rights. Adoration is opposed to, is the opposite of, overweening human pride. We acknowledge God as infinitely perfect and know ourselves as finite, passing away like the grass of the fields, which today is green and lush and tomorrow is burned up.

Dom Prosper goes on to say that nothing is more important than adoration and urges that the act should not be a passing thing but should be turned into a habit. One cannot think, he says, that it is appropriate at one moment and not at another. The eucharistic preface reminds us at every celebration of the Eucharist that 'It is very meet, right and our bounden duty that we should at all times and in all places give thanks unto thee, O Lord, holy Father, almighty, everlasting God.' The Latin words were *semper et ubique* – always and everywhere. If we live our lives in the daily, hourly knowledge that it is in God that we live and move and have our being, then adoration should arise in us at once. It should be, as we might say today, the default position. And in this sense – I quote Dom Prosper again – adoration should not be an effort, for, given our existence and God's existence, it comes so to speak by itself.

Guéranger draws particular attention to one word in his definition: he said that adoration is a loving act. We know what this means if we have looked at someone lovingly. Adoration is not something sterile or dry in which the heart has no part. It is our response to an attraction; the attraction causes it to arise. The creature puts itself in its right place, that is in its relation to the Creator. The creature puts itself in its right place and is happy to be there, and more than that – how shall we put it? – God finds it to his liking. It is beautiful in his eyes. And as the lover looks upon the beloved in a relationship of mutuality so God enters into a more complex relationship with those who have made adoration habitual. Dom Prosper's language, albeit in translation, has a freshness and an unfamiliarity to it: 'If God has been familiar with certain of his creatures, it is because they had acquired, from adoration, something that enraptured and seduced him. And so there is nothing more important, nothing wiser, nothing truer than adoration.'

The focus of our specific act of adoration at the feast of Corpus Christi is Christ, the incarnate Son of God, in his sacramental eucharistic presence. This is just one instance of adoration, and a specifically liturgical and sacramental one, but we can adore anywhere and at any time – whenever, being alert to God's love, we are aware of it, we should lift our hearts, with sweetness and with ease. If we can do so before the Blessed Sacrament, so much the better. Dom Prosper concludes, 'As long as one knows God, one can adore, and God has put at the disposition of everyone the means to know him. And so, it isn't a question of something wise or clever . . . it is a thing God expects of you and in which you will find your soul's rest.'

CORPUS CHRISTI:
THANKSGIVING FOR HOLY COMMUNION
Therefore we before him bending

And so we come to the end. This is a festival day, a day of triumph and of celebration. Processions have been a feature of such a day since the beginnings of human history, and few occasions would have been more glorious than those in which the victorious Roman general enjoyed his triumph, his procession of honour through the streets of the provincial capital or through Rome itself. On this day of *Corpus et Sanguinis Christi*, the Body and Blood of Christ, it is Christ who is the victor; it is his triumph; it is he whom we honour in songs of praise and, in many places, in the procession of the Blessed Sacrament.

A triumph was not any everyday affair in ancient Rome; it was, by definition, exceptional and different. Corpus Christi too is exceptional and different. When the office and Mass of the feast were compiled by St Thomas Aquinas in the thirteenth century, the antiphons, responses, hymns and prayers that were spread across the day formed a unity. They moved the participant from thanksgiving for ordinary daily food through the accounts of the gift of manna from heaven to the Israelites in the wilderness and the feeding of the five thousand by Jesus to the institution of the Holy Communion itself and Christ 'giving himself with his own hand'. The procession and the blessing, the benediction, given with the sacrament, were one part of this great whole.

Aquinas not only conceived today's feast – a feast that originated, as we saw, in the eucharistic devotion of nuns in Liège in the late twelfth century – as an act of thanksgiving and of adoration, but as an occasion in which we who participate should be enabled to contemplate the nature of the Eucharist.

The familiar motet O *sacrum convivium* is really the Magnificat antiphon for second Vespers: that is to say, the verse sung before and after the Magnificat at medieval Evensong.

It sums up, in a most memorable way, the four elements of the Eucharist. It is a feast, a sacred banquet, in which Christ is received, in which we are permitted to eat his flesh and drink his blood, as real food and real drink. It is a solemn memorial of Christ's saving death: as we take the bread and wine, we proclaim the Lord's death until he comes again. It is an occasion of grace: our minds, our hearts, our very beings, are filled with the grace, mercy and love that pours from God through Jesus Christ. And it is a pledge, a promise, an anticipation of what is to come, of a glory that we will share with Christ, as today we share his triumph, of a communion in which we will participate forever, the communion of saints.

Week by week we celebrate the Eucharist and receive it as the sustenance needed for daily living and spiritual growth. Today, we return our thanksgiving to God for this great gift, the sacred banquet wherein Christ is received, the memorial of his Passion is celebrated, the mind is filled with grace, and a pledge of future glory is given us. Alleluia!